Critical Thinking For Leaders

Ben Garrido

Shinasc

Contents

Your First Day

01

Main Questions	What kinds of challenges will you face when you become a professional?
	How can you prepare to lead students?
	How can you prepare to deal with customers?
	What can you expect of your bosses?

Vocabulary	Devotion	Punk
	Petitioner	Power Struggle
	Dealing with ~	Overwhelming

Welcome to Work

Congratulations! You have passed your professional test! Maybe you are a teacher, now. Maybe you're a public official, maybe you're a social worker. Regardless, it's been hundreds of hours of hard work, studying all night and memorizing grammar. You have **devoted** years of your life to this day and it is a great accomplishment.

However, your challenges are not finished. Some of your bosses will be wonderful, and some of your coworkers will become good friends, but not all of them. The following story is a kind of worst case scenario, but you will almost certainly face some of these problems.

You enter your new workplace for the first time. You breathe deeply and open the doors to your office. If you're a teacher, you will see your new coworkers for the first time. One of them is sitting alone in the corner drinking coffee. He looks annoyed. Two teachers are looking at a cartoon on a computer screen. The first gently puts her hand over the other teacher's shoulder as they laugh. The teacher next to your desk is more than 60 years old. The supervisor is late to work.

You say hello and the coworkers all greet you. They are friendly, but you feel like there is tension between some of them. You get several invitations to dinner. You'll have to choose one group of people to meet and you don't know how to decide. This seems **overwhelming,** so you prepare your work alone.

Your first student will come into class. He is early. He is eager to talk to you and sits next to your desk, asking lots of questions. You tell him to wait while you prepare and he seems disappointed. Another student comes in and he sits alone in the back of the classroom. Over the next twenty minutes most of the students come into class. The bell rings and you begin teaching.

This first boy who comes to class is full of enthusiasm. He wants to answer all of your questions, he won't stop raising his hand. The quiet boy still hasn't looked at your eyes. Just as you are getting ready to practice your first drill, four students come late into your class and talk loudly, disrupting all the other students.

You finish the day's classes and go back to your office. You want to ask the vice principal how to deal with the loud, late students but he is outside smoking a cigarette. As you wait for the vice principal to return, you get your first call from a mother.

"My son was late to your class today," the mother says. "I'm very sorry. He's so wild and bad I can't control him. Yesterday I found out he was stealing my things! I want you to control him very strictly, but don't make him sad. I hate it when my son is sad."

You agree to try and hang up. How on earth are you supposed to be strict without making the boy sad? You think about how crazy this mother sounded and think no wonder her son is a ***punk***. The vice principal is still outside smoking a cigarette when you get another call.

"Hello," the second mother says. "My son came to your class early today. He wanted to practice English with you, but you were too busy. He is feeling disappointed because the class was too easy. Is there anything you can do to help my son?"

You say that you will find something and hang up. You remember the quiet boy who wouldn't look at you. You worry about him and call his mother's phone number. She doesn't answer. The vice principal is still smoking. As your first day at work ends, you have to choose a group of teachers to have dinner with. As you get home late that night you are very tired. You go to sleep knowing that the next day, there will be more challenges.

Moving to to another country won't help. Growing up is hard and all people, from all countries, are going to have struggles in during childhood. Indeed, compared to Canadian or American students, Korean students are really good.

If you are a public official, the situation won't be that different. There will be political struggles, there will be difficult **petitioners,** there will be unreasonable customers who want impossible things. Any position of leadership, whether you are leading students or managing public services or helping a business become more efficient, will challenge you every single day.

How can you survive in these complicated, imperfect environments?

Workplaces Are Complex

One of the first things you should understand is that workplaces are really, really complex. They are twisted nets of human relationships. You will be in the middle of hundreds of **power struggles.**

Students will struggle with other students, they will struggle with you and they will struggle with their parents, sometimes all at once. If you show weakness, these people will absolutely take advantage of you. Your coworkers will struggle against each other. They will make and break friendships. They will struggle against students, you and their bosses. Your bosses will struggle against each other, against you, against your co-workers and against parents. Then there are parents, who are often unpredictable, impossible to please and in conflict with everyone else.

Then there are the problems you will face in classrooms. Students are not very predictable. For example, you might prepare a class about Albert Einstein because your most brilliant student loves Einstein. Then, when you get to class the next day, your brilliant student doesn't want to talk because he just had a fight with his sister. The quiet boy might tell you that he is afraid of his brother or that his grandmother is sick. The students who come late and talk loudly will sometimes change suddenly, becoming studious. This happens all the time - some of my best college students were bad students in middle school and some of my most accomplished coworkers were kind of wild when they were younger.

If you go into business, you will find that customers are similar. Many customers are very happy to take all of your attention so that you can never help other customers. Some workers will require lots of attention and some will want you to leave them alone. Some are lazy, some are afraid, some of them are going through divorces. Your bosses will change their minds unpredictably. Sometimes they will make you change and then blame you when those changes don't work.

If you want to be a good leader, you must learn how to adjust to all of these changes. You will need to develop strategies for **dealing with** parents, customers, bosses, coworkers and students. This will not be easy but, if you succeed, the rewards are incredible.

Questions

Exploration

- What kinds of problems did you cause for your teachers and/or bosses?
- Bosses often hold you responsible for their decisions. How can you deal with this problem?
- Many parents only care about their own children. You have to care for all the children. How can you negotiate with these parents?
- Laws change all the time. How can you deal with shifts in official policy?
- How should you handle rivals?

Cooperative Exercises

- Ask a friend what he/she thinks the most important skills are for a good leader.
  - ____
  - ____
  - ____
- What attitude should you have on your first day? Ask a classmate.
  - ____
  - ____
  - ____
  - ____

02 The Rewards

Main Questions	Leadership is hard. Why do people do it?
	How have teachers affected your life?
	How important are your leaders?
	How much power do you have?
	What are the differences between good and bad bosses?

Vocabulary	Life Satisfaction	Shepherd (verb)
	Meaningful	Abstract
	In Essence	Reform

Last chapter I made teaching or managing people sound like a pretty horrible job. It is hard, but it's also one of the most rewarding and **meaningful** jobs a person can have. If you are a teacher or a public official, you will be dealing with people all day, every day. It's not like accounting or logistics. You will not waste all your time talking to computers. You will not spend all day doing paperwork. You will instead spend a lot of your day shaping human lives.

I am writing this textbook because I had an amazing teacher in my freshman year of high school. Before I met that teacher, I really had no idea how to think. I am living in Korea because of an excellent history professor who showed me how amazing Asia could be. I got my first good job because an excellent business manager convinced me to try newspapers. I got my current job because I had a really good boss who encouraged me to pursue graduate school.

And it works in reverse, as well. A former student of mine recently called to thank me for helping him get into a good university. Another former student wants to write a book with me. Dozens more still send me Facebook messages and chat with me on KakaoTalk. I feel really, really good when these things happen.

Mattering For People's Entire Lives

According to a study by economists Raj Chetty, John N. Freidman and Jonah E. Rockoff[1], a good teacher's influence lasts decades. Students who have good teachers are more likely to go to college, more likely to earn good money and less likely to have teen pregnancies. Conversely, having a bad teacher is as bad for a student as skipping most of a semester. Students suffering from bad teachers only learn about 30% as fast as students with average teachers.

Managers are similarly important. According to Business Insider Magazine[2], a good manager can make an unproductive worker as productive as an excellent worker and a bad manager can make an excellent worker perform like a terrible

1 Impact of good and bad teachers. http://obs.rc.fas.harvard.edu/chetty/value_added.html

2 Effects of good and bad managers on productivity. http://www.businessinsider.com/managers-have-an-even-bigger-effect-on-productivity-than-we-realized-2013-1

worker. And managers don't just have an impact on their workplaces. According to The Atlantic Magazine[3] bad managers can cause heart disease, family problems and chronic stress. However, good managers can improve the **life satisfaction**, health and family stability of their workers.

Furthermore, you will be the center of attention when you lead. Every single person in the classroom will be watching you, listening to what you say. Every single person in that meeting room will assume you have important things to tell them. You will command people every single day.

If you are a teacher, not only will you command hundreds of people, you will be shaping them at the most sensitive times of their lives. According to Alex

3 Mangers' impacts on workers' health. http://www.theatlantic.com/health/archive/2012/02/the-impact-of-bad-bosses/253423/

Brooks of Kidspot[4], you will be **shepherding** 5-8 year old children through the intuitive phase, when they begin to form basic logic and social skills. You will teach these children how to read and understand, how to speak and express themselves. Then you will be responsible for helping them with the concrete operations stage, age 8-13, where they begin to learn adult problem solving and then the formal operations stage, 13 years and up, when they really become adults. Middle school and high school students will come to you to learn how to use **abstract** logic and do moral reasoning. They will, **in essence**, be asking you to help them build an adult identity. You will help these children form their moral codes, their ways of thinking and their ability to reason.

Confucius wrote that there is no hope for reforming a bad person older than 40, and it is true that people generally become less able to change with age.[5] As such, it's important that we help people develop when they are still young. However, even if we can't change those older people easily, we can still impact their lives. Whether you are a teacher, a manager or a public officer, impacting lives is your job. If you do it well, your goodness and power will be felt for decades.

---

4 Development of cognition in children. http://www.kidspot.com.au/discoverycentre/Development-Development-Cognitive-development-in-babies-and-children+5357+553+article.htm

5 The critical period hypothesis seems to support Confucius. http://www.lel.ed.ac.uk/~jim/crit.per.pdf

Questions

Comprehension

- What is the intuitive phase?
- What is the connection between managers and health?
- How can leaders impact other people?
- How much damage can a bad teacher do?
- How much good can a good manager do?

Exploration

- Which teachers have made the biggest impacts on your life?
- Which managers or bosses have changed your life the most?
- How did they help you or hurt you?

Cooperative Exercises

- With a friend, list the characteristics of your ideal boss.
    - ______________________________
    - ______________________________
    - ______________________________

- Speak with classmates and collect ideas for how to positively shape people's lives.
    - ______________________________
    - ______________________________
    - ______________________________
    - ______________________________

The Value of Critical Thinking

03

Main Questions	Do people learn faster when they memorize or think critically?
	Should training programs be boring or entertaining?
	Why is context important for learning?
	What are the best ways to build motivation in students or employees?

Vocabulary	Dreaded Self	Default Self	Ought Self
	Ideal Self	Rote Learning	

Many teachers and managers believe that critical thinking is a good thing, but impractical. After all, every minute you spend thinking about something is a minute you can't spend memorizing facts or information about your products. However, there are a number of scientific reasons to believe that critical thinking is actually more efficient than memorizing in many situations.

Critical Thinking vs. Rote Learning

According to Dr. Robert Bjork, all learning is contextual. Whether you are teaching students, educating the public or training employees, there will be a social context, an environmental context, a body context and even your mood context for every new thing learned. Changing the context, Dr. Bjork said, changes the way the memory gets saved in our brains. As such, you should explain things in realistic, practical contexts. There is some research that suggests learning the same thing in different contexts is good for memory.[6] For example, learning how to drive on a computer simulation, in a textbook, on a country road and in the city is often more efficient than learning in just one way. This means that when we learn a new thing, we have to integrate it within the system of things we already know. Just like bricks in a wall, we need to make information fit in our memories.

Let's explore how this concept of contextual memory works. "51384," for example, is difficult to remember and has almost no meaning by itself. In **rote learning,** I would just memorize the numbers. However, if I connect those numbers to another concept, a date, it becomes much easier to remember. 51384 becomes May 13, 1984. This is much easier to remember, but it's not very meaningful. But if I connect it to a third concept, my birthday, it's almost impossible to forget. "May 13, 1984, my birthday" is easier to remember than "May 13, 1984," and they are both easier to remember than "51384."

6 Dr. Robert Bjork on contextual learning. http://gocognitive.net/interviews/effect-context-memory

So, how can we encourage contextual memory? Critical thinking is a very efficient method.

There's also the nature of memory. As you can see below, learning is a circle, leading to and from short term memory, to and from long-term memory.

MULTI-STORE MODEL

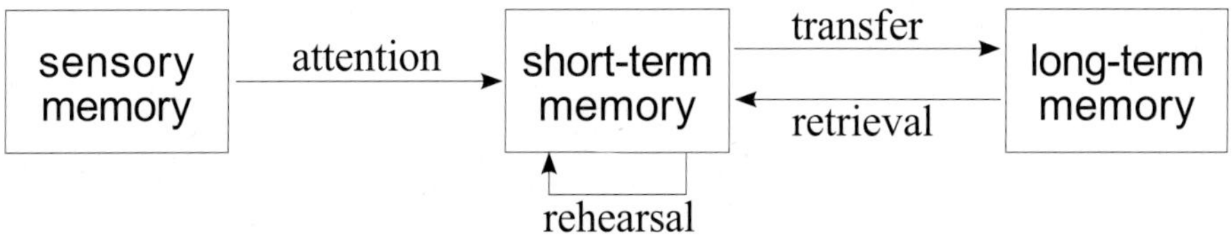

To explain how short and long term memory work, imagine you are playing a game of baduk. When you consider your opponent's previous moves, remember the specific strategy you plan to use and attempt to predict your opponent's next move you are using short term memory. It's where your memories do work. It's where you update and change memories.

This is all good, but in order to win your game of baduk, you need to retrieve memories about lots of game strategies. You also need to remember what strategies your opponent used in the past. Maybe you can guess his intentions better if you have a memory of the things he said before the game. Maybe you can remember your game strategies better when you connect them to your favorite songs. These long-term memories are in the background of your consciousness, but you aren't actively using them.

The thing about memory, however, is that the more you use it the stronger it becomes. The more people move long-term memories into short-term memory, the more often people save short-term memories in their long-term memory, the better the understanding and retention of the fact. Thus, if you want to train or teach effectively, you should encourage learners to retrieve and store memories regularly.

So how can we encourage learners to move memories back and forth from short to long term memory?
Critical thinking is one very efficient method.

Beyond memory, another very important factor in how efficiently people can learn is motivation. Demotivated learners don't work as hard, they quit easily and they don't learn in context. Poor motivation, in other words, will absolutely kill your lesson, presentation or training program.

It seems clear that a manager, teacher or public official will need to understand motivation if they want to be effective. As such, we need to investigate the best ways to create motivation in students, trainees or the public.

According to motivation researcher Zoltan Dornyei, motivation originates in imagining the future.[7] Dornyei theorizes four dimensions to motivation, four ways to imagine the future. The first is the **ideal self**. This is when people imagine the best possible outcomes. For example, if a worker imagines that learning English will help her get a promotion, attract a rich and handsome husband, please her parents and improve her understanding of life, she will be very motivated to learn English.

Second is the **dreaded self**. This is where people imagine the worst consequences of

7 Future selves model of motivation http://www.zoltandornyei.co.uk/

failure. If a student imagines that failing to learn accounting means he will get fired, break up with his girlfriend and be diagnosed with cancer, he is going to be very motivated to learn accounting.

Third is the **default self**. This is what people think is likely to happen. Fourth is the **ought self**, which is what the person's family, friends and society think they should do. A default example might be something like "I think I have a good chance to get a job after I graduate." An ought self might be something like "my parents will be so proud if I get a promotion" or "I should try hard so that my friends aren't ashamed of me."

The really interesting thing about this kind of motivation is that the more vivid your imagination, the deeper your thinking, the more powerful your motivation. According to Teresa Garcia and Paul Pintrich[8], there is a consistently positive relationship between motivation, making strategies for the future and the depth of critical thinking.

Critical thinking is serious business.

As such, helping your students or employees think critically and creatively is not a "fun distraction" from "real" education or "real" training. It is the most efficient and important teaching you can do.

8 Critical thinking and motivation http://eric.ed.gov/?id=ED351643

Questions

Comprehension

- What is the future selves model of motivation?
- How is learning contextual?
- What is the circle of memory?

Exploration

- What kinds of activities have you experienced that helped you think critically?
- What motivates you? Try to answer in terms of Dornyei's future selves model.
- How can you develop your imagination?
- Why do you think that so many classes and training sessions are built around memorization?

Writing Activity

- Very few successful people are boring. Very few interesting people lack imagination. Why do you think that is?

____

____

____

____

____

____

____

Ways to Encourage Critical Thinking

Main Questions	What is more important, a conclusion or the process of reaching a conclusion?
	How can you make students or employees care about your goals?
	Should you express your strong opinions to your followers?
	Should you listen more to people who are very certain about their beliefs?

Vocabulary	Editorialize	Process	Defensive
	Ambiguity	Open Ended Questions	

Now that we've established the value of critical thinking, we need to discuss how to encourage that critical thinking. I'd like to recommend asking open ended questions, emphasizing **process** over results, developing tolerance for **ambiguity** and resisting the urge to **editorialize.**

Don't Editorialize and Emphasize the Process

Minimizing the importance of your own opinions is, in general, a pretty good idea. If you are trying to get students, coworkers or employees to think critically, it's even more important to minimize your own opinions. So, what do I actually mean by that?

Good critical thinking is a process, not a result. It is far more interested in understanding an issue than finding conclusions. Your opinion should not get in the way of this exploration. Let me give you an example.

Let's pretend I believe guns should be legal for normal people. If I start a by expressing my belief, it is almost impossible for others to think critically about the issue, much less have an interesting conversation. If I announce that "I strongly believe guns are good for society. Let's have a discussion," it's very unlikely to be a useful discussion. The reasons it likely won't be a good discussion are as follows:

1. People who disagree with me will likely feel uncomfortable.
2. People who disagree with me will likely feel **defensive** and want to argue.
3. People who agree with me will feel empowered and stop listening to others.
4. People without a strong opinion will likely want to avoid the discussion.

Expressing strong opinions makes it hard to have a good discussion.

In other words, when I say "I strongly believe guns are good for society," I have made everyone uncomfortable, defensive and aggressive. The odds that anyone will think critically about my opinion are very low. The odds that we will have a useful discussion about guns is even lower. I have, basically, made an awkward family dinner with your craziest uncle.

So, what happens if I try again but keep my opinion secret? What if I say, "I'm really interested in your thoughts on guns." If the person says they support guns, I can continue the discussion by asking why or I can ask why other people disagree. If the person says they don't support guns, I can ask questions like, "some people feel really strongly about this issue. Why do you think they support/don't support guns?"

By asking **open ended questions** and keeping my opinion secret I'm encouraging people to talk comfortably. When they are comfortable, they are much more likely to continue the conversation, much more likely to consider new ideas and much more likely to learn from the experience. Whether you are a teacher, an office manager or a public official, you will need people to consider new ideas and learn from their discussions with you.

The ruler must not reveal his views. For, if he reveals his views, the ministers will display their natures differently. If the likes and hates of the ruler are concealed, the true hearts of the ministers will be revealed.
-Han Fei-tzu, Tao of the Sovereign

So remember, a discussion is far better than simply expressing your opinion, the process of finding a conclusion is far more important than getting the conclusion you like best and critical thinking only happens when people feel comfortable. Keep your opinions flexible, open to revision and mostly hidden if you want to lead a healthy classroom, office or company.

Open Ended Questions and Ambiguity Tolerance - Tips for Encouraging Critical Thinking.

Students will sometimes disagree with your beliefs. If you want to create an environment of critical thinking and dynamic learning, that has to be okay with you. Here are two general strategies to help.

First, try not to be too certain about your opinions. Life is big and complicated and if you really think about it, the honest answer to most questions is "we don't know." While not knowing is scary to most people, but it's also the best path to learning. If you are too certain of your opinions you literally cannot learn.

As such, I suggest that you actually think about the limits of your knowledge. How much do you really know about your favorite song, for example? Do you actually know how to make your favorite food or how to grow a tomato? Do you have any idea how your shoes were made? If you don't know even these simple things, can you really be sure about much more complicated things like religion, politics or morality? I think that, if you're honest, you'll admit that you can't be sure.

Getting comfortable with uncertainty is called ambiguity tolerance. It is a type of honesty and is a type of humility. When you admit that you don't know everything, you can make your students or coworkers more comfortable and you can have much better conversations. After all, if you aren't sure, it's not a big deal when your students, coworkers or employees have different opinions.

The second technique is to ask open-ended questions. Most people like to talk. If you want to make them comfortable enough to engage in critical thinking, help them to talk. Avoid yes/no questions and instead use questions the other person can answer at length.

The only true wisdom is knowing that you know nothing.
- Socrates.

Good things to say for critical thinking:
Why do you think so? / How did you come up with that idea? / Do you think ~ is an emotional decision? / How does ~ make people feel? / Can you describe ~ more so I can understand? / I wonder about ~

Bad things to say for critical thinking:
Aren't you wrong? / That's dumb, isn't it? / I strongly believe ~ / I think we all agree that ~ / Everyone knows ~ / I don't want to hear about ~ / Yes or no.

Use Dilemmas

A dilemma is a decision with no clearly correct answer. It can be something as simple as "should I drink liquor tonight, have fun and then feel bad tomorrow" vs. "should I not drink liquor tonight and feel better tomorrow?" It can be as serious as Sophie's Choice[9].

Regardless of what kind of dilemma you choose, a dilemma will help both you and your students/coworkers to tolerate ambiguity, think critically and learn efficiently. In the next two chapters you are going to experience a dilemma. After you've experienced how a dilemma feels, you will learn how dilemmas are structured, how to make them and how to modify them.

9 Sophie is a fictional character who had to decide which of her two children to protect from the Nazis.

Questions

Comprehension

- What is a dilemma?
- What negative things happen when you express a strong opinion?
- What is ambiguity tolerance?

Exploration

- When was the last time you had a really good conversation? What were the characteristics of this conversation?
- Conmen and dishonest people in general often use certainty to fool others. Why is certainty so powerful?

Project

- There are pictures of Socrates and Han Fei-tzu in this chapter. Pick one of them. If you choose Socrates, explain why he distrusts certainty. If you choose Han Fei-tzu, explain why he thinks leaders should not express their opinions.

05 Admiral Lee Sun-shin's Hidden Dilemma

Main Questions	How did King Sejong's policies irritate the nobility?
	Why did King Seon-jo and the nobles view Lee Sun-shin as a threat?
	Why wasn't Joseon prepared for the Imjin War?
	How much loyalty should you show an incompetent leader?
	Did Lee Sun-shin make the right choice?

Vocabulary	Meritocracy	Incorruptible	Emissary
	Cannon	Tactics	Delusional

You are all familiar with the great admiral Lee Sun-shin. He really did do most of the amazing things you saw in the movie, Myeongnyang. He really did defeat hundreds of Japanese warships with his panoksun and turtle boats. He really did save Joseon from almost certain destruction. In his personal life, he was basically a Confucian superhero. However, like most heroes, his life was a lot more complicated than you probably realize. To understand why, let's start with King Sejong's **meritocracy** and the Literati Purges (사화) that followed.

Sejong the Great Upsets the Nobility

Let's pretend that my father is much more powerful than your father. Maybe my father is a judge and your father is a construction worker. However, while you are an excellent piano player, I'm not able to play piano very well. We both go to a piano audition to become professional pianists. Who will get the job?

In modern Korea, if there is an opportunity to be a professional pianist, you will almost certainly get the job instead of me. The reason is that modern Korea believes in meritocracy - that we should choose talented and skilled people. But we have not always believed in meritocracy.

Sejong the Great hired people like Jang Young-shil because he valued ability more than family connections. The nobles hated him for this.

Indeed, one of the main reasons a nobility exists is to stop talented people from competing with high-born people. In Lee Sun-shin's lifetime, for example, a bad piano player with an important father almost always beats a good piano player with an unimportant father. If the good pianist with the unimportant father did somehow get hired, the nobles would often just kill the good pianist.

King Sejong, who of course lived a century before Lee Sun-shin, was a meritocrat. He continually promoted and hired people based on their ability. Talented people from unimportant families like Jang Young-shil achieved great power under Sejong. Because so many people of ability had power, Joseon became powerful and rich during Sejong's time.

However, because Sejong kept giving important jobs to people with merit, the nobles could not get the important jobs. As such, many hated and opposed Sejong. When the great king died, these nobles worked to get their power back. They began a program called the Literati Purges (사화). One of the goals of the Literati Purges was to kill talented people. That way, if all the talented people were dead, nobody could challenge the nobles.

Jo Gwang-jo believed in giving power to the best people so the nobles killed him.

You probably already know about famous Literati Purges figures like Jo Gwang-jo, but the important result of the Literati Purges is that many of these smart and talented people either died or ran away to the countryside. The nobles were so successful that by the time of Lee Sun-shin's life, the nobles were very powerful and meritocracy was almost completely dead.

Seon-jo, Hideyoshi Toyotomi and Lee Sun-shin - Dangerous Times

Hideyoshi Toyotomi and the Japanese invasion force.

Lee Sun-shin began his career fighting a group of barbarians called the Jurchen (여진나라) in North Korea, near the Chinese border. He soon became famous for two things, fighting the Jurchen very well and being **incorruptible**. We need to explain why that's important.

In modern Korea, success and honesty would be useful for our careers. However, Joseon was a society controlled by nobility. Lee Sun-shin's commanders and King Seon-jo saw that he was popular and successful and so they had him arrested and tortured. After all, if successful and popular people are alive, maybe they will challenge the nobles.

To prevent this danger, King Seon-jo and the nobles promoted corrupt and incompetent military officers to replace Lee Sun-shin. The corrupt and incompetent officers might not be able to fight the Jurchen, but at least they would make Seon-jo and the nobles look good by comparison.

Around this time, the late 1580s, Japanese leader Hideyoshi Toyotomi was trying to decide on a strategy for conquering China. He had two basic options. He could attack from the south, moving through Joseon and into China. He could also attack from the north, landing his forces in Manchuria (만주). In order to make this decision, he started talking with Seon-jo. He asked for permission to land in Korea and attack China, but Seon-jo said no.

Seon-jo then sent **emissaries** to Japan to decide if Toyotomi planned to attack Korea anyway. One emissary said "there is no danger. Toyotomi is not going to attack Korea." The second emissary said "oh my God! Toyotomi is going to attack us very soon!"

If Seon-jo had been a smart king, he could have sent more emissaries to find out for sure. He could have prepared for the worst and strengthened the military. He could have sent spies or tried to negotiate with China. He could have negotiated with Toyotomi. However, Seon-jo was one of the worst leaders in history and so he decided to stop talking with Toyotomi and reduce the size of the Joseon military. "If Japan attacks our powerful country, it will be like a snail falling on a rock," he said. [10] In other words, "Japan is so weak and we are so powerful that I don't care."

The only good thing Seon-jo did around this time is let Lee Sun-shin out of prison. Lee Sun-shin did not agree with Seon-jo's strategy of ignoring dangerous enemies and making the country weak so he disobeyed Seon-jo and prepared South Jeolla Province for war.

We learned earlier that most of the smart people in Joseon had either died or run away. One of the places many of these talented people went was South Jeolla Province. Lee Sun-shin recognized this and, instead of fearing them like Seon-jo or the nobles, used them to prepare South Jeolla Province.

---

10 The War Diary of Yi Sun-shin http://www.goodreads.com/book/show/3146909-nanjung-ilgi

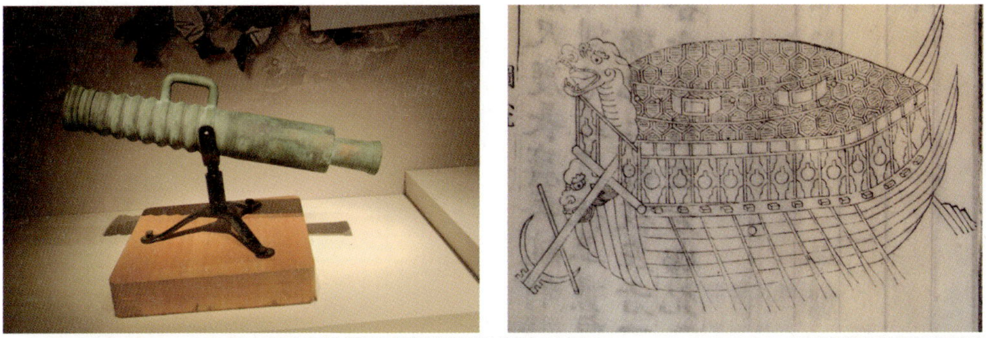

The cannons and turtle boats Lee Sun-shin used were mostly designs from King Sejong's time.

These smart people helped Lee Sun-shin restart King Sejong's old weapons programs, redeveloping things like the turtle boats and the best **cannons** in the world at the time. They also helped him store extra food, build defenses in the South Jeolla cities and train farmers to be soldiers. As a result, while the rest of Joseon was very unready for war, South Jeolla Province was a very strong, very prepared region.

Seon-jo's Decisions and Lee Sun-shin's Heroism

Seon-jo's belief that Japan was too weak turned out to be false. In 1592, the Japanese landed in Busan. The local commanders were so incompetent they didn't figure out there had been an attack until Japan controlled the entire city. From there, it only got worse for Joseon. The Korean military that Seon-jo had weakened was no match for Toyotomi's professional soldiers. Japanese forces completely destroyed entire Joseon armies and burnt dozens of cities to the ground. They reached Seoul in only a few months. Faced with this danger, King Seon-jo bravely ran away, abandoning the people of Seoul to the Japanese.

The Japanese were winning easily. In fact, they really only faced one problem - getting food and supplies to their armies. The roads from Busan to Seoul were really bad, but that didn't seem like a big problem. Toyotomi would just send the food and supplies on ships from Busan, around Jin Island and up to Seoul.

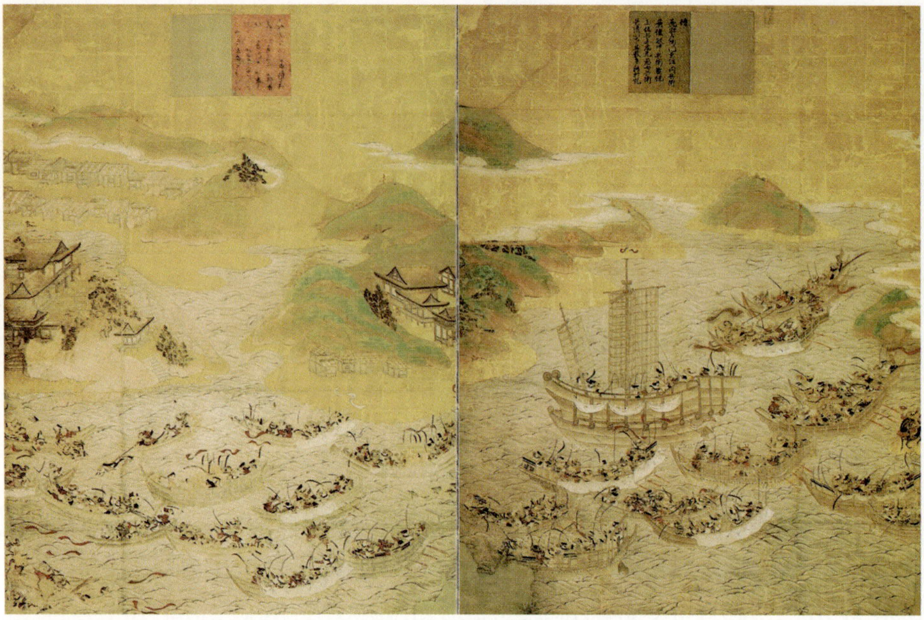

What could possibly go wrong with sending ships to Jeolla Province?

Unfortunately for him, that meant sending boats through Jeolla Province, where Lee Sun-shin and the only prepared soldiers in Joseon were waiting. Really unfortunately for Toyotomi, Lee Sun-shin and the people of Jeolla Province had invented a whole new type of warfare. Instead of ships fighting at close range with arrows and small guns, Lee Sun-shin's new type of war focused on shooting at ships from long range with advanced cannons. This new type of war would devastate the Japanese navy.

Lee Sun-shin Stops the War, Seon-jo Restarts the War

From 1592 until 1594, Lee Sun-shin and the people of South Jeolla Province systematically destroyed the Japanese navy. The turtle boats and panokseon that Admiral Lee had developed were vastly superior to the Japanese ships, but Lee Sun-shin's battle **tactics** were also excellent. He tricked the Japanese into traps many times and never allowed the Japanese to take favorable positions. Lee Sun-shin was a careful, brilliant military leader who deceived and confused the Japanese at almost every battle.

Because of Lee Sun-shin and the people of South Jeolla Province, the Japanese Army, which was still easily destroying the Joseon forces, ran out of food and supplies. Toyotomi had to stop the invasion and go back to negotiating with Seon-jo.

Toyotomi wanted to end the war, negotiate safety for Japanese people living in Busan and leave Joseon alone. Seon-jo negotiated for a while, but by 1597 Seon-jo had decided it would be best to attack the Japanese people living in Busan. Seon-jo and the Chinese emperor also decided that Toyotomi was a weak and defeated king who wanted to become their "servant." Toyotomi, for some reason, also decided that China was surrendering to him. Since all three leaders, Toyotomi, Seon-jo and the Chinese Emperor, were making **delusional** decisions the war restarted in 1597.

By this time, Lee Sun-shin and the people in South Jeolla Province had built a large and powerful fleet of ships, 133 turtle boats and panokseon. Seon-jo, taking advice from a Japanese spy, wanted to use this fleet to destroy the Japanese navy. Lee Sun-shin, however, knew that this "opportunity" was a trap and disobeyed King Seon-jo's order. King Seon-jo responded by locking Lee Sun-shin in prison and torturing him again.

Lee Sun-shin had been popular, successful and good at his job - one of those meritorious people the nobles don't like. As such, Seon-jo decided to replace him with a corrupt and incompetent general named Kwon Yeol. Kwon Yeol promptly sent all 133 ships into the Japanese spy's trap. 120 of the ships were destroyed. A huge number of Joseon's best sailors died. Because of Seon-jo and Kwon Yeol, the Korean navy was reduced to only 13 ships.

King Seon-jo bravely panicked and asked Lee Sun-shin to rescue him from the Japanese, again. Lee Sun-shin accepted, left prison and disobeyed King Seon-jo's order to abandon the navy. He led those thirteen ships in his most famous battle, Myeongryang. Once more, he destroyed the Japanese navy and saved

Joseon. The war continued for another year, and Admiral Lee Sun-shin died in his final battle. He had fought the Japanese 23 times and won each time. He had saved Joseon twice. He was also probably lucky to have died, because there's some evidence in the War Diaries that Seon-jo and the nobles were planning to torture him more after the war.

The Aftermath

The Imjin War was an absolute disaster for Korea. Seon-jo remained king for another decade. He did not learn very much from his mistakes and he didn't not improve much as a leader. Approximately 35% of the Korean population had died during and after the war. Millions died in the invasion and millions more died from disease and starvation.

Many of the smart people who had survived the Literati Purges either died during the war, moved to Japan or were kidnapped by Toyotomi. While the Japanese were forced to leave, the Chinese took advantage of Seon-jo's weakness to occupy and exploit the country. The Joseon dynasty went into steep decline and never recovered.

Lee Sun-shin was a brilliant admiral. He was smart and honorable and inventive. He tried to stop the war by remaining loyal to his incompetent king. However, his decision to remain loyal to Seon-jo resulted in a massive disaster.

Those who cannot remember the past are doomed to repeat it."
-George Santayana

Questions

Comprehension

- What were the Literati Purges?
- Why did Lee Sun-shin get arrested and tortured so often?
- Was the Imjin War a success for Joseon?

Exploration

- Lee Sun-shin was pretty obviously better than his bosses. How do you deal with incompetent bosses, teachers or leaders?
- Find out why Jo Gwang-jo was forced to commit suicide. What does his death say about the Literati Purges?

Role Playing

- Form a group with three students. One student should roleplay as Toyotomi, one should roleplay as Seon-jo and one should roleplay as Lee Sun-shin. How would you behave differently in the same situation?

06 Erwin Rommel, The Desert Fox

Main Questions	What was blitzkrieg?
	Did Rommel make a good decision?
	How did Hitler ruin the defense of France?
	Why didn't Rommel take the Suez Canal?
	How much loyalty do you owe bad leaders?

Vocabulary	Artillery	Daring	Infantry
	Territory	Compromise	Unworthy

Field Marshal Erwin Rommel, better known by his nickname "The Desert Fox," is one of the most famous figures of World War Two. While he has many interesting and unique qualities of his own, we are mostly interested in him here because his career closely follows the career of Lee Sun-shin. Like Admiral Lee, Rommel was an excellent military leader. Like Lee Sun-shin, he was respected by both his countrymen and his enemies. Like the Korean war hero, Rommel was honorable, incorruptible and very brave. Also like Lee Sun-shin, Erwin Rommel had an ineffective and horrible boss.

Hero of WWI

Erwin Rommel joined the German army from a young age. In his twenties, he graduated from the military college and became an **artillery** officer. During World War One, Rommel really showed his potential. He was one of the first people to develop techniques based around speed and aggression.

He was also very good at tricking his enemies. Once, in Italy, Rommel managed to capture 9000 enemy soldiers. He did this by attacking from strange positions, attacking when his enemies weren't prepared and by making his force look much larger than it was. The enemy officers, when they surrendered, were very surprised that Rommel only had 150 soldiers. Largely because of Rommel's skill in deception, these enemy generals had believed they were fighting the entire German army.

Rommel insisted on personally leading his soldiers on these **daring** attacks. He was wounded several times and nearly died. Still, Rommel never asked for a safer job and never let others take risks for him. By the end of the war, Rommel had become one of the most famous people in Germany.

The Battle of Caporetto, where 9,000 Italian soldiers surrendered to Rommel's 150 soldiers.

Rommel Devastates France

German tanks race through France.

Between World War One and World War Two, Rommel asked to transfer from **infantry** to commanding a tank division. Rommel believed that he could use his quick, aggressive, attacking strategy from World War One more effectively with tanks. He was right.

Rommel was one of the first people to use a new tactic called "Blitzkrieg," which means lightning war. Similar to the way Lee Sun-shin invented cannon based naval warfare, Rommel fought his tank battles with the idea that you should never let your enemy prepare or rest. When Germany attacked France, Rommel led an incredibly successful campaign.

His division, nicknamed the "Ghost Division" for their extreme speed and effectiveness, raced across France at record speed. They captured as much as 400 kilometers of **territory** per day. Really think about that, travelling from Busan to Seoul is only 325 kilometers. Rommel travelled farther than that in one day while fighting the French army.

Rommel partially succeeded because he could move so fast the French could never prepare a defense. However, he also partially succeeded because he had a habit of ignoring Hitler's orders. This made him unpredictable for the enemy.

Once again, Rommel led his soldiers from the front. He was wounded several more times in World War Two, but he never asked to go somewhere safer.

Africa, Hitler's Disastrous Decisions and Return to France

After destroying France, Hitler and the Germans sent Rommel to North Africa. The reason they did so is because the Italians, allies of the Germans, were getting badly beaten by the British. Even though Rommel was outnumbered, he continued his string of victories. He beat the British many times and came very, very close to taking control of the Suez Canal.

Rommel's tanks in North Africa.

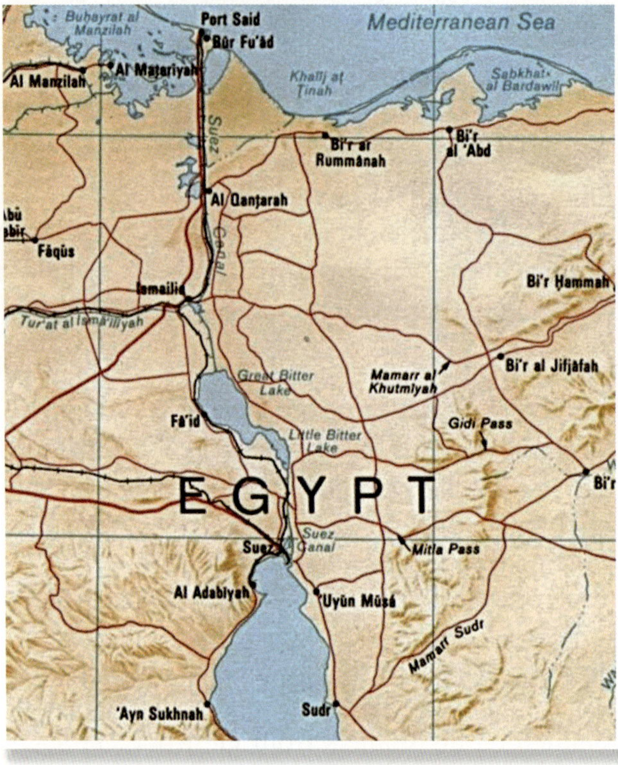

The Suez Canal goes through Egypt

It's important to understand just how important control of the Suez Canal was. The Suez Canal allowed soldiers, supplies and trade to move from the Mediterranean to India, East Africa and much of the Middle East. Had the Germans taken the Suez Canal, they could have cut off British and American access to oil, troops and dozens of important ports. The Germans could have probably removed 2,500,000 pro-British Indian soldiers from combat, taken control of huge oil fields and, possibly, won the war.

Rommel recognized this and asked Hitler to give him more soldiers and gasoline. "We have an opportunity to win the war, please give me more supplies." Hitler, who was by this time taking large doses of a drug called methamphetamine, rejected Rommel's request. Instead of taking control of the Suez Canal, Hitler took away Rommel's supplies and soldiers so that he could attack Russia.

Rommel had to give up trying to take the Suez Canal and retreat west. The attack on Russia, which Hitler thought was more important than the Suez Canal, resulted in total disaster. The campaign resulted in the deaths of more than 2,500,000 German soldiers[11], the devastation of Germany's tank divisions and no long term gains.

During the disastrous invasion of Russia, Hitler was also busy making horrible decisions in Africa. He ordered Rommel to concentrate on killing Jewish and black civilians - Rommel ignored these orders - instead of preparing for British and American attacks. When Rommel retreated to Tunisia, he sent a message to Hitler explaining that he didn't have enough weapons, soldiers, fuel or food to fight any more. Rommel wanted to retreat to Europe and prepare a defense of Germany, but Hitler told him to simply fight the Americans and British until all the German soldiers had died. Rommel disobeyed this order as well, but not before the Americans and British had destroyed a large percentage of his army.

After the disasters in Russia and Africa, Hitler ordered Rommel to prepare a defense of France. Rommel did a good job preparing the defense but had a problem with the tanks. Most of the German generals wanted to put the tanks far away from the beaches of northern France. This way the tanks would be safe from airplane attacks and the Germans could attack the Americans and British after they landed in France. This idea was logical and could have worked.

Rommel wanted to put the tanks right next to the beaches. That way, if the Americans and British attacked, the tanks could stop them from getting into France at all. The American and British planes could attack these tanks, but it would have been very difficult for British or American soldiers to directly attack Northern France. This idea was logical and could have worked.

Hitler, however, had a different idea. He wanted to **compromise** between Rommel and the other German generals. Hitler ordered the tanks to stay a "medium" distance from the beach - close enough for American and British planes to attack, far enough away the tanks couldn't fight. This was an incredibly stupid decision. The American and British airplanes had no problem finding and destroying German tanks and then, when they attacked France, the surviving German tanks were too far away to do anything.

11 http://russia-insider.com/en/history/wwii-3-out-4-german-kia-were-soviet-army/ri6663

It became more and more obvious that the Germans could not win World War Two. Rommel and many of the other generals wanted to negotiate with the British and Americans to end the war. They hoped that by doing so, they could protect Germany from the Soviet Union and stop killing so many German soldiers for no reason. Hitler, though, had a different idea.

Hitler explained that he was basically perfect and that the German people had failed him. "If the German people lose the war, they will have shown themselves **unworthy** of me," he said.[12] Therefore, Hitler planned to fight until everyone had died. This would be a good because then the German people would be punished for "failing" Hitler.

At this point, Rommel and several other German officers decided that it would be best to kill Hitler. They arranged a plan to kill him with a bomb but the bomb wasn't strong enough. Hitler quickly discovered that Rommel was a part of the assassination group.

Rommel and several other German officers tried to kill Hitler in this room. Hitler survived.

12 http://www.bbc.co.uk/history/worldwars/wwtwo/hitler_russia_invasion_01.shtml

Aftermath

Hitler forced Rommel, his best general, to commit suicide as punishment for the assassination attempt. Despite the fact Germany had no hope of winning, Hitler continued the war for another year. This resulted in the deaths of more than 10,000,000 people. Because Hitler wouldn't negotiate with the Americans and British, the brutal Soviet Union took control of half of Germany. British, American and Soviet airplane attacks erased entire German cities. By the time Hitler committed suicide in 1945, almost all of Germany had been destroyed.

Rommel was a brilliant general. He was smart and honorable and inventive. He tried to stop the war by betraying Hitler. His decision to betray Hitler resulted in a massive disaster.

Questions

Comprehension

- What did Rommel do at the Battle of Caporetto?
- What is blitzkrieg?
- Why didn't the Germans take the Suez Canal?

Exploration

- Erwin Rommel was vastly better than Hitler. Should he have obeyed Hitler just because Hitler was his leader?
- In the modern world, Nazism is considered extremely evil. Why, in the 1930's, did so many people support the Nazis?
- Do you think Erwin Rommel and Lee Sun-shin were more similar or more different?

Role Playing

- Make groups of two. One student should roleplay as Hitler, one should roleplay as Rommel. How would you behave differently in the same situation?

Who Made the Better Decision? 07

Main Questions	What is the most difficult dilemma you have ever faced? How did you solve it?
	How can businesses, schools or governments use a devil's advocate?
	Is it better when everyone agrees to a solution easily?
	Is it useful to argue in favor of things you don't believe?

Vocabulary	Strategic	Legitimate	Devil's Advocate
	Groupthink	Immune	

I think there are a lot of similarities between Erwin Rommel and Lee Sun-shin. Rommel was probably one of the three best army commanders of World War Two[13] and almost all people would agree that Lee Sun-shin was the best commander of the Imjin War. Both men had a reputation for honor and honesty. Lee in particular was famous for being completely incorruptible[14] and Rommel was well known for honorable treatment of prisoners and civilians - providing free medicine to conquered cities and refusing Hitler's orders to kill commandos or POWs.[15]

Both men were incredibly brave and both got the absolute respect of their soldiers. Both succeeded by developing new ways of fighting wars, canon-based distance warfare in Lee's case and Blitzkreig in Rommel's case. Both were incredibly deceptive and **strategic**. Lee's use of tides and rope traps in the battle of Myeongnyang is one of the most incredible deceptions in military history. Rommel's incredible "Lightning Attack" of France is still the fastest conquest in history.

Unfortunately, they both also ended their lives in similar ways. Lee was loyal and died for his loyalty. He won but Joseon was still ruined. 35% of the population had died and there was a Chinese occupation. The literati were mostly dead or hiding in Japan. Seon-jo continued his incompetent rule for another 10 years. It was, by any measure, a complete disaster for Joseon.

Rommel was disloyal in an attempt to save Germany and died for his disloyalty. Millions more Germans, Russians, Americans and Englishmen would die as the war needlessly continued for another year. Germany was almost completely destroyed, with entire cities erased. The Americans and British conquered the western half of Germany and went to work erasing German culture. The Russians conquered the eastern half, where countless German civilians were raped and murdered by vengeful Soviet troops. It was, by any measure, a complete disaster for Germany.

---

13 Soviet General Georgy Zhukov and American General George Patton had similar levels of skill compared to Rommel.

14 If you read the War Diary of Yi Sun-shin (난중일기) you will be shocked at how incredibly corrupt Seon-jo's officials had become. That Admiral Lee never became corrupt in such a corrupt environment is a tribute to his honesty.

15 Rommel was deeply insulted when the Americans tried to assassinate him in 1943, not because they tried to kill him, but because they sent the assassin to a safe house far away from the fighting. Rommel was annoyed the Americans thought he would hide in such a safe place. He did become friends with the assassin, though.

So we really can't judge Rommel or Lee on results because they both died and left disasters in their countries. Lee Sun-shin supported King Seon-jo until his death, despite the fact that Seon-jo was a terrible leader. Rommel betrayed Hitler and attempted to kill the legal ruler of his country. This choice, betray or support the terrible ruler, is the major difference in their military careers or, at least, the major difference we are interested in.

Since we can't really judge them based on the results of their decisions, we have to instead judge them on their process. Should a soldier remain loyal always, even when his boss is stupid, dangerous and destructive? If so, how can we ever get rid of terrible leaders? Should a soldier betray his bad boss, even when that boss is the **legitimate**, legal ruler of the country? If so, how can we ever have stability when soldiers can betray any leader they don't like?

If this seems like a difficult question, it is. There is no "right answer" and there is no obvious way to decide. You are going to have to think hard. You are going to have to wrestle with a dilemma. In order to do this, I suggest you learn how to play **devil's advocate.**

The Devil's Advocate

When you search for the term "devil's advocate" in online dictionaries, you will find a technically correct but unusual definition. The word comes from the Catholic Church and their process for making saints. Maybe if you understand the history of the word, you can understand the concept better.

In the Catholic Church, the devil's advocate's job is to always argue against the saint. Even if all the priests and cardinals think that someone should be a saint, the devil's advocate will argue against them. The Catholic Church doesn't do this because they like to have arguments, but because they think that the devil's advocate will help them avoid prejudice, groupthink and bad information. After all, if there is a mistake in the priests' beliefs about a saint, the devil's advocate will find that mistake. If the priests are not thinking clearly, the devil's advocate will attack their bad argument.

Catholic priests debate whether or not to make a new saint.
One of these people would have been "the devil's advocate."

The most interesting thing about the devil's advocate, though, is that they often don't believe their own arguments. Very often, in the devil's advocate's opinion, the person should be a saint. However, they still argue against the saint because they believe arguing helps everyone understand the issue more clearly.

These days, most devil's advocates aren't involved in the Catholic Church. Most of the smartest companies and governments assign people to play devil's advocate when they make important decisions.[16] It can be very dangerous to make

16 Using devil's advocates in business decisions. https://www.ideals.illinois.edu/bitstream/handle/2142/29170/

Where you most often find the devil's advocate in modern times.

decisions without a devil's advocate because when everyone agrees, there is no reason to search for bad thinking or faulty information. An extreme version of this is called **"groupthink."** Groupthink is behind many of the world's most disastrous decisions.[17] No culture or country is **immune** from groupthink.[18]

As such, I would like you to practice playing devil's advocate. I'd like you to ignore your own opinion and make arguments for both Rommel's decision and Lee Sun-shin's decision. In other words, make sure you can logically and convincingly support both loyal Admiral Lee and disloyal Field Marshall Rommel. Only after you've made a good argument for both men can you chose who you think made the better decision.

useofdevilsadvoc1036schw.pdf

17 What is groupthink? http://www.psysr.org/about/pubs_resources/groupthink%20overview.htm

18 Examples of groupthink in industry. http://www.happycampus.com/doc/11249662

Questions

Comprehension

- Why did the Catholic Church use devil's advocates?
- What is groupthink?

Exploration

- Find a specific example of groupthink and explain what happened.
- Find a specific corporate or government use for devil's advocates.

Exercise

- Choose one of the following unlikable positions and make a convincing argument supporting it.
    - *The military draft is okay because only young men get drafted. Young men are the most disposable people in society, so it's okay if they die.*
    - *Societies with more educated women have higher divorce rates. Therefore, we should stop women from getting education.*
    - *Slavery was useful for the development of society. Without slaves, education, science and art would never have advanced. As such, slavery was a good thing. (Check Hannah Arendt if you need help.)*
    - *Some cultures and religions are simply evil. We should force people from these evil cultures and religions to change.*
    - *We should destroy books, movies and art with bad morals. Things like violent cartoons and sexual music videos should be banned. If people are allowed to think bad things society becomes too dangerous.*
    - *Laws are unnecessary. We should just appoint very moral people to be judges. (Check Confucius if you need help.)*

Structure of a Dilemma

08

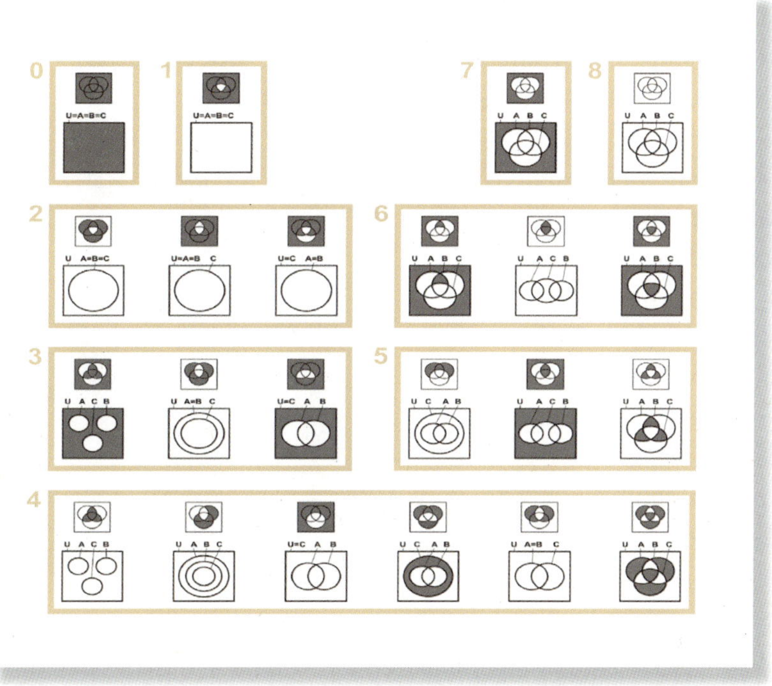

Main Questions	What are the three kinds of dilemma?
	How are dilemmas useful for teaching or training?
	How should you lead a dilemma?
	Why is ambiguity tolerance desirable?

Vocabulary	Infamous	Ambiguity	Counter-argument

Were the stories about Admiral Lee and Field Marshall Rommel more interesting than some of the other history that you've learned? If so, I think that is because some history classes are full of rote lessons where students are supposed to remember unconnected facts and memorize the "official opinion."

The stories in this book about Lee Sun-shin and Erwin Rommel, by comparison, were about critical thinking and good narrative - which you'll learn about later. There was never an opinion about who made the better decision. There was never an attempt to give you an answer. Indeed, the opposite was true. I tried to write the stories so you could argue against any common opinion. In other words, I structured those two stories as a dilemma.

That dilemma was designed to stimulate the vivid imagination that Zoltan Dornyei (the motivation researcher from Ch. 3) thinks is so closely linked to motivation. It was designed to put you in a situation that demanded critical thinking. It was designed to help you remember and it was designed to help you more deeply understand the meaning of the stories, rather than just the names and dates. It was designed to help you experience dilemmas as an educational or training tool.

Structures of Dilemmas

The most important characteristic of a dilemma is that there is no obviously right answer. Every dilemma will have different answers for different people. You can achieve this through three basic structures.

Dilemma type one:

Good Action → Bad Result

This is any time that doing a morally good action leads to a bad outcome. There are an infinite possible number of variations on this structure, but the following example is fairly typical.

Jane is a policewoman who walks into a building as sees an **infamous** serial murderer attacking a victim. It is clearly morally good for Jane to help the victim, but if she does so, the serial murderer can escape and murder more people later. In dilemma type one, Jane protects the victim from the murderer (morally good action), allowing the murderer to escape and kill more people (bad outcome).

Dilemma type two:

Bad Action → Good Result

This is any time a morally bad action leads to a good outcome.
Just like the first example, Jane walks into a building and sees the infamous serial murderer attacking a victim. However, Jane realizes that the murderer can escape if she helps the victim and, this time, she makes a different decision. Jane lets the murderer kill the victim (morally bad action), but this gives the other police enough time to catch the murderer and prevent future murders (good outcome).

Dilemma type three:

Amibiguous Action → Ambiguous Result

This is the most complicated type of dilemma and also the most common type of dilemma people face in the real world. You can recognize this type of dilemma any time a morally ambiguous action leads to a morally ambiguous outcome.

For example, Lee Sun-shin remains loyal to a horrible leader (morally ambiguous action) and saves his country, but at horrible cost (ambiguous result).

For another example, Rommel betrays a terrible leader (morally ambiguous action) for the chance to end Hitler's crazed government, but knows the consequences of failure will be very severe (morally ambiguous outcome).

The Leader's Role in Dilemmas

The leader's ultimate job during a dilemma is to encourage discussion. In order to do this well, the leader should prepare the following strategies.

1. The leader can argue against all of the students/employees. This is an example of devil's advocate behavior. The leader should use this strategy when the students or employees don't know how to be a devil's advocate.

Leaders working through a dilemma .

2. The leader can encourage his/her followers to present all possible opinions by themselves. In other words, the leader asks the students or employees to ignore their own opinions and focus on understanding all of the opinions. This is generally fun and good for communication. The leader should use this strategy when the employees or students already understand how to be a devil's advocate.

However, whichever strategy the leader chooses, he or she should prepare the dilemma carefully. Dilemmas, and critical thinking in general, require much more work from the leader than a lecture would.

The first challenge is getting the correct attitude. The leader must tolerate **ambiguity.** If the teacher is too immature and needs "the right answer" they will ruin a dilemma by forcing an opinion on the employees or students. If there is a "right answer," there is no longer a need to think. In order to keep this tolerance for ambiguity, I strongly recommend the leader never actually expresses their opinion. In other words, the leader's belief should be a secret.

As for preparation, the leader needs to anticipate all likely answers. To use our stories as an example, the leader should have good reasons why Lee Sun-shin was correct AND good reasons why Rommel was correct. The leader should prepare **counter-arguments** for all possible answers.

Lastly, the leader should choose an interesting or important topic that isn't too difficult. We will discuss how to do this in chapters 14, 15 and 16.

You must NOT fall in love with your own opinions. You must NOT forget to make someone into a devil's advocate. You must NOT forget that ambiguity is a good thing for critical thinking.

Questions

Comprehension

- What is ambiguity tolerance?
- What is the fundamental characteristic all dilemmas share?

Exploration

- Can you think of any real life dilemmas you've dealt with?
- Search for "the prisoners' dilemma," "catch 22" and the "trolley problem."

Activity

- Write one example of each of the three types of dilemma.

- Practicing your ambiguity tolerance and devil's advocate skills, lead a different student through one of your dilemmas. Write down what the other student says.

Tools For Evaluating Decisions

Main Questions	Have you ever thought about your moral assumptions?
	Is it okay to just use your intuitions when making moral decisions?
	What are the basic moral assumptions of your religion?
	Are "good and bad" real things?

Vocabulary	Assumption	Subjective	Golden Mean
	Veil of Ignorance	Categorical Imperative	Propriety
	Harmony	Moral Relativism	

Many dilemmas and critical thinking decisions come down to moral evaluations. In order to help students or employees build good systems for moral thinking, you need to understand your own moral **assumptions**. Unfortunately, many people never do this even once in their lives.

The truth is that unexamined morality is **subjective**. It's just a feeling or a set of prejudices or a group of habits. Because of this, the first thing a critical thinker must do is choose their basic moral assumption. Once the basic assumption is chosen, then the critical thinker can start making logical rather than emotional decisions about morality. To help you start out on this path, I've prepared a list of moral systems along with their assumptions and criticisms.

The Golden Mean (중용)

Kongzi, philosopher of the golden mean.

This idea comes from several different cultures, most famously by scholars in the Confucian tradition and by Aristotle and his followers. Aristotle used bravery as an example. Too little bravery is cowardice and cowardice is bad. Too much bravery is recklessness and recklessness is also bad. It is only when we use a medium amount of bravery that we achieve courage and goodness. This idea assumes that badness comes from extremes and that good comes from moderation.

You can find this idea in Christianity, Judaism, classical Greek philosophy, Buddhism' s "middle way," Confucianism's "doctrine of the mean" and also in Islam. The golden mean is often associated with ideas of beauty, virtue and sophistication. Confucianism, for example, says that the golden mean is necessary if you want to become a "superior man."

Criticisms of the golden mean: The most obvious criticism is that "medium" is subjective. An action that seems very extreme to you might be normal to me. For example, in 8th century Arabia you could get the death penalty for stealing another person's water. This was because in 8th century Arabia, it was very hard to get water in the desert. In 21st century Korea, the death penalty would be a very extreme punishment for stealing water, but it could be normal in different contexts.

Another problem is the idea of extremes. Is it wrong, for example, to be extremely educated? Is it evil to be extremely good at soccer or extremely bad at singing? Some philosophers think that "good" should be independent from the idea of extremes. If good is independent of extremes, then the golden mean is wrong.

The Veil of Ignorance (무지의 베일)

A veiled man.

Imagine there are only four possible types of life. You and three other people each have a 25% chance of being a king/queen, a 25% chance of being a public official, a 25% chance of being a laborer and a 25% chance of being a slave. In the veil of ignorance, you and the other three people would then negotiate the rules of your society. Whatever you decide is "good."

This system was invented by an American philosopher named John Rawls. He thought that if people could not know their position in society - maybe they are kings, maybe they are slaves - then they would make all the positions fair. Evil is only possible when people know their positions in society because it is only then they can take advantage of others.

Rawls gave the example of slavery. When the slave owners know that they will be slave owners, they can invent lots of reasons why slavery is good. They can use religion, science, traditions and thousands of other reasons. However, if there was a chance they could become slaves, they would stop supporting evil things like slavery naturally. A slave owner can only be evil if he knows he will be a slave owner and not a slave.

The veil of ignorance is commonly used in economics. Similar ideas were also used in the Age of Enlightenment. The veil is still very important for social contract theory.

Criticisms: The first problem with the veil of ignorance is that we can never really forget what our social position is. We have to pretend we're ignorant, but we still know. This means we can never reach the ideal "ignorant" condition.

The second problem is that even if we could become perfectly ignorant, people still might be prejudiced. For example, maybe I hate laborers. I hate them so much that I think they should be put in jail. My hatred is so strong that I will punish laborers even if I have a 25% chance of being a laborer. There are a lot of examples of this type of prejudice. 50 years ago in Korea, most people would choose to arrest homosexuals even in the veil of ignorance. 120 years ago in America, most people would help Gompers and Gutstadt persecute Asians. 500 years ago in France, most people would choose to punish Jews, Muslisms and Buddhists, even in the veil of ignorance.

Immanuel Kant

The Categorical Imperiative (정언 명령)

This is probably the most common moral system right now. It is the morality you learn most often in middle and school ethics classes. Invented by Immanuel Kant, the first part says that we should only do an action if we would be alright with every other person doing the same things. Simpler, this means "if you wouldn't be satisfied when other people did this thing, don't do it." Doing something to another that you don't like is evil. Doing something that you do like to another person is good.

The second part says "act in such a way that you treat humanity, whether in your own person or in the person of any other, never merely as a means to an end, but always at the same time as an end." This means that it is evil to use people like tools.

The third part of the categorical imperative says that you should pretend that all of your actions are universal law. This idea is very similar to the Christian idea that you should "do unto others as you would have them do unto you."

Criticisms: The categorical imperative does not care about results. For example, in the categorical imperative, it is wrong for Erwin Rommel or Lee Sun-shin to force a soldier to fight because that is using the soldier like a tool. However, if we can't use soldiers like tools, it is very difficult to survive. Indeed, the categorical imperative does not allow you to hurt one person a little bit to help a lot of people.

Another example is lying. It is wrong to lie because allowing everyone to lie would be a terrible universal law. Now, imagine that a scared man comes to your house and says "I'm hiding from a murderer, please let me hide in your house." You agree and let him hide in your house. Then the murderer comes to your house and says "I'm looking for a scared man. Did you see him?" Under the categorical imperative, you cannot lie to the murderer because lying is wrong.

Confucius

Propriety

This is the most common system of traditional Korea. Propriety means "humbling yourself and honoring others." It focuses on group cohesion (화합) more than individual rights. Confucius believed that "good" was **harmony**, like in a happy family. When people use propriety their goal is to make others happy. If we always focus on other people's happiness we can avoid selfishness, cruelty and ambition. Confucius' ideas are the most important moral forces in the histories of Korea, China and Japan, but they were also important in the European Renaissance.

Criticisms: Some people think that individuals cannot trust groups of people to make them happy. Therefore, if we use propriety and other people don't, we get cheated constantly. Indeed, in the history of China, very Confucian emperors often had horrible problems with other kings, nobles and countries taking advantage of them.

Further, if we only focus on making other people honored and happy, we cannot fight evil. In summary, some people say that propriety makes it too easy for bad people to hurt good people.

Moral Relativism

Margaret Mead was an important anthropologist who helped popularize moral relativism.

Moral relativism says that right and wrong come from our childhoods and our cultures. For example, it is morally wrong for a Jew or a Muslim to eat pork but for a Buddhist or Christian, eating pork is fine.

Moral relativism comes mostly from anthropology. Anthropologists in the early and mid 20th century began studying many different cultures in places like the Amazon Jungle and tiny Islands in South Asia. They found that moral behavior was always different. For example, in some societies, it is very immoral and cowardly if men refuse to let village elders cut their skin. In other societies, it is considered respectful to eat your enemy's body. Even in modern countries like Korea and England, morals are different.

Imagine there are a group of loud, drunken old men in a coffee shop. They are cursing and bothering everyone. In Korea, it is moral to endure the drunk, cursing old men and respect them because they are old. If a young person confronted the old men, it would be very disrespectful. It would be even worse if the young person made the older men leave. In England, on the other hand, it would be considered immoral and cowardly if the younger people didn't make the obnoxious older men leave.

Criticisms: If everything is determined by culture, there is no way to judge a culture's morals. For example, in Mexico 400 years ago, the Aztecs believed it was moral and normal to sacrifice thousands of people in religious festivals. In the 1930s, Japanese people believed it was their moral duty to destroy and replace the "broken" cultures in Asia. The members of ISIS honestly believe it is right to kill people who are not Sunni Muslims.

If we say that morality is dependant on culture, how can we criticize the Aztecs, Japanese or ISIS members? They were simply doing what their cultures said was moral and we should accept them, right?

Questions

Comprehension

- What is propriety?
- What is the categorical imperative?
- What is moral relativism?
- What is the veil of ignorance?
- What is the golden mean?

Activity

- Choose your favorite moral system and use it to evaluate Lee Sun-shin and Erwin Rommel.

  ____
  ____
  ____
  ____
  ____
  ____
  ____

- Choose your least favorite moral system and use it to evaluate Lee Sun-shin and Erwin Rommel.

  ____
  ____
  ____
  ____
  ____
  ____

What is Narrative?

10

Main Questions	What is narrative?
	How can teachers use narrative to engage students?
	How is a narrative created?
	What is the relationship between logic and good stories?

Vocabulary	narrative	Abstraction
	fictional elements	contextual learning
	formula	rote learning

Introduction to **Narrative**

Stories are fun. Sure, they have all kinds of important, serious uses psychology, politics and even mathematics rests on narrative foundations but we'll worry about things later. For now, let's focus on wizards, monsters and princesses.

Our bodies can't visit Mars or use magic, but we can do anything in a story. Because **narrative** is just anything that logically connects things and events, almost anything can become a narrative. **Fictional elements** are fine. If you want werewolves and zombies, narrative is a great tool. Your imagination is the only limitation. Ghandi can learn French cooking with an alien supermodel, Dracula can become a ballet dancer and your mother can operate an international spy organization if you want.

Fantasy is not the only way narratives are fun. Stories are how humans make sense of the world. They are how we understand good and evil. Without narrative words like "father," "love," and "fear" become empty **abstractions**. Every time you remember your grandmother, you are making a narrative in your head. Every time you get angry about injustice, you are making a narrative to explain that anger. Every time you imagine your dreams, you put those dreams in the context of a story.

Narrative is a powerful thing. It attracts people or repels them. It is the difference between enjoying Harry Potter and being miserable while doing taxes. Narrative is the foundation for most important decisions. Your justification for life is a narrative.

Narrative in the Real World

Let's try an example of just how important narrative is to leaders in general and teachers in particular. Imagine there are 100 freshman college students who need a philosophy class for liberal arts. They can choose between two instructors.
The first instructor is Professor Kim. He knows all the philosophers' names and memorized all their ideas. He was a good student in graduate school and has published many academic papers in philosophy journals.

He specializes in Greek philosophy. Professor Kim studied Greek because he wanted to be a better expert. He has read all of the works of Aristotle in the original Greek and checked the exact meaning of each word Aristotle wrote. He is currently working on a project to check the exact meaning of every word Plato wrote.

He says that his goal is to understand all of the individual words written by all of the Greek philosophers. He isn't worried about the overall meaning of Aristotle or Plato's books, but thinks that being 100% accurate is a good goal.

The second instructor is the famous director Park Chan-wook. He is also a philosophy major but his main job is a movie director. His three most famous movies were made to explore revenge.

In the last of his revenge movies, Sympathy for Lady Vengeance, an innocent girl named Geum-ja goes to jail for twenty years because of a corrupt policeman. When she gets out of jail, she devotes her life to revenge. Geum-ja starts wearing red eye shadow and leather clothes. Eventually, she catches both the policeman and the real murderer and tortures both of them. At the end of the movie, Geum-ja has gotten her revenge but realizes that she is now as guilty as the original murderers.

Caption: Left to right - Park Chan-wook really is a philosophy major.
Poster for Sympathy for Lady Vengeance.

In magazines, Park has explained that he was interested in the philosophy of revenge. He wrote and directed his revenge movies because he wanted to emotionally understand the pain and destruction that revenge causes.

Between Professor Kim and Park Chan-wook, who would the liberal arts students choose? Most of the students will probably pick Park Chan-wook. They probably think he is more fun. They might believe that his class will be more interesting. They might also feel guilty for choosing Park Chan-wook's fun class. Maybe they think that learning should be painful and awful. Maybe they believe that education works better when it's dry.

This woman is not ready for learning.

Students might choose Professor Kim because they think he is more knowledgeable about philosophy than Park Chan-wook, even though they are both philosophy majors. Perhaps some students will think that being a movie director isn't really connected with the ability to teach philosophy.

I think those students are wrong. I would be shocked if students didn't learn more from Park Chan-wook than Professor Kim. Why? Because Park Chan-wook is good at narrative and Professor Kim isn't.

Narrative is just logically connecting things and events with other things and events. This means that Park Chan-wook's stories are fun partly because they are logical and systematic . Sympathy for Lady Vengeance connects ideas about revenge, suffering and, the best ways to live in ways that people can understand. Park Chan-wook builds systems of thought instead of just throwing random, unconnected facts at you. Using systems of thought is called **contextual learning**. Using random facts is called **rote learning**. Contextual learning tends to be vastly more efficient.

Professor Kim, because he is interested in individual words and doesn't try to make a story out of Aristotle or Plato, is much less likely to teach students efficiently. By focusing on details and ignoring context, Professor Kim makes it extremely difficult to remember facts. Because he only cares about the individual words Aristotle wrote, he makes it almost impossible for students to learn the actual meaning of Aristotle's books. He is also unlikely to understand Aristotle himself.

Anything that logically connects things and events is a narrative.

A narrative can be a film or a book or a comic, which is what most people normally think when they hear "narrative." Films have passionate kisses (events) and angry bosses (things). Books have characters (things) searching (events) for lost treasures (things). Comics have heroes (things) and villains (things) punching each other (events). In good films, books and comics, the kisses happen for clear or interesting reasons, the treasure is important to the story and the villains have believable motivations for fighting the heroes. In bad films, books and comics, things seem to happen for no reason. Characters are difficult to believe or unrealistic. Conflicts feel unnatural or stupid.

However, these are not the only types of narratives. Instruction manuals are narrative. The law is a narrative. Math can be a narrative.

The **formula** below is the narrative of a plant turning light, water and CO2 into sugar - photosynthesis. More important for us, good leaders are good storytellers. Now that we know what a narrative is, let's make one.

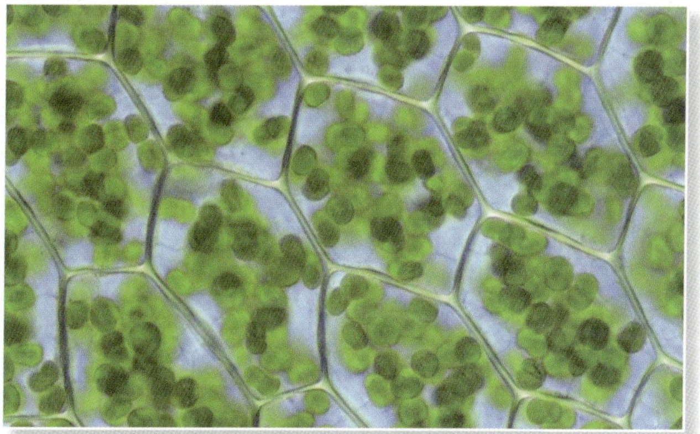

Caption: $6CO_2 + 6H_2O$ (things) — sunshine → (event) $C_6H_{12}O_6 + 6O_2$ (things)

Question:

Take a moment and look at the following pictures. Make quick notes about whatever you notice.

These pictures are tools to help you build your own narrative. Please pick one person and one place. Then, after you've chosen, make a narrative to explain what the person is doing in the place. If you want to choose an unusual combination, like the ballerina on Mt. Everest, that's perfectly fine. If you want to create additional characters, go for it. Whatever you choose, take twenty minutes and write a story about your character and your setting. Save this story, as we'll use it throughout the book.

11 Why Leaders Need to Be Good at Narrative

Main Questions	What are the central religious, historical or mythological narratives of your culture?
	What, in your experience, is the most powerful type of narrative?
	Where does human empathy come from?
	How can narrative make learning more effective?

Vocabulary	Meaning	Mirror Neurons
	Cognitive Processing	Empathy
	Critical Thinking	

Storytelling is Human Nature

There are huge differences between cultures. In some Amazonian cultures, it is a sign of respect to eat your enemy's body. In Ancient China, young women achieved beauty by breaking bones in their feet. In some Native American cultures, boys became men by piercing their skin with wood hooks and then hanging from trees.

It's not just exotic cultures that have unusual beliefs. The Hwaryang of Goryeo believed that homosexuality made soldiers into better fighters. Some American Christians play with poisonous snakes to show their faith in God. The English still say "Hello Magpie" seven times when they see a certain kind of small bird.

However, even with all this variety, there are a few things that all cultures do. Storytelling is one of these things. Every culture has a story to explain its origins. All cultures use stories to teach religion, history and morality. Every culture has heroes and villains. The reason for this comes from the actual structure of the human brain.

From left to right - The Japanese landing at Busan, Napoleon Bonaparte riding his horse, Jesus dying on the cross. These stories are how people understand really important things like the Imjin War, the nation of France and Christianity.

The brain makes sense of the world by organizing information into stories. In this way, facts connect with other experiences and emotions to create **meaning**. The more connections a fact has, the more narrative surrounds a fact, the better we can remember that fact. More importantly, the more narrative surrounds a fact, the better we can use this fact.

Facts without narrative context are almost useless.

Human beings, and a few other animals, have special cells called **mirror neurons** that give stories immense power. According to the American Psychological Association, mirror neurons allow one person to share an experience with someone else.[19] For example, if you are hungry and see a person eating cake, you will salivate. You will immediately imagine the cake in your mouth. You will taste the person's cake in your mind.

This ability to enter another person's mind comes from mirror neurons and it is a huge part of what makes us human. It seems to form the basis for **empathy**. Or, in other words, mirror neurons seem to be a major reason human beings are capable of social activity.

I mention this because narratives are a very powerful way to stimulate mirror neurons. In a 2010 study by the National Academy of Sciences[20], scientists did brain scans to a storyteller and an audience member at the same time. They found that the listener's brain would sync up to the storyteller's brain during the story. This is a fancy way of saying that the storyteller was putting his mental-state directly into the listener's brain.

The storyteller can thus engage the listener with not just facts, but biochemically and emotionally. This creates the opportunity for very rich, very efficient learning. Students in storytelling environments, by syncing up with the teacher's brain, bond more easily with the teacher. Mirror neurons can even sync the brains of the audience with fictional characters, which is one reason fiction is so powerful.

19 Mirror neurons. http://www.apa.org/monitor/oct05/mirror.aspx

20 Brain syncing. http://blogs.discovermagazine.com/80beats/2010/07/27/study-the-brains-of-storytellers-and-their-listeners-actually-sync-up/#.V_3MrsnMiVs

Caption: Mirror neurons in action. Baby macaque brain-syncing with a human scientist.
(Source Evolution of Neonatal Imitation)

Storytelling environments also help students use their imaginations and think creatively. Further, storytelling helps students connect new facts with their personal experiences. All of these things have been linked with improved memory, **critical thinking** and vocabulary. Just teaching facts, by comparison, is unnatural and difficult for **cognitive processing**. It's also extremely boring.

Perhaps most interesting, the power of the storyteller and audience connection depends on the quality of the narrative. Good narratives showed very strong connections between the storyteller and the audience. Bad narratives showed weaker connections.

Most people agree that leaders are powerful influences on their followers. However, because of mirror neurons and storytelling, we now know that a good storytelling leader doesn't just teach a student, trainee or dependent, that leader actually enters the person's mind.

Questions:

Comprehension:

- What are mirror neurons?
- Why is storytelling a powerful way to affect students, trainees or followers?

Exploration:

- Think back to Professor Kim in Ch. 10. Why is he unlikely to be a good teacher?
- Many educators believe that students learn best when they are bored and unhappy. Why do you think this is?

Activity:

- Talk with another student. Describe a narrative (movie/book/comic/etc) they don't know. Then have the student describe an unfamiliar narrative to you. How similar are your moods and feelings after you finish describing the narratives?
- What kinds of narratives did your best teachers use? What kinds of narratives did your worst teaches use?

Worst Teachers	Average Teachers	Best Teachers

Concrete Details

12

Main Questions	Have you ever experienced a good narrative about a topic you don't like?
	Do you enjoy abstract theories?
	How do you feel when a fictional character you like gets hurt?
	How can you use narrative to make others interested?

Vocabulary	Concrete	Description
	Reflection	Generalization
	Mere Description	True Narrative
	Endeavor	Sync

I am going to describe a keyboard. I am doing this because a keyboard is the least interesting thing I can think of, and describing it with good narrative will be a challenge. I will try it three times - once with abstractions and generalizations only, once with concrete details and once with a combination of **concrete** details and conflict. See which one gets your attention the most.

Description One:

"The keyboard is black with white letters on each key. It is a little bit shiny. It measures 33 centimeters by 20 centimeters. It transfers information from my fingers to the computer, allowing me to type. It is useful for a writer."

Is this even a little bit exciting? Probably not.

But now let's play with this **description**. Find a keyboard and tap on it. What sort of sound comes out? Is it hollow or solid? Imagine the little mechanisms hidden under each key. Imagine the little springs and pieces of rubber. Are the keys old and smooth or are they new and textured? How does your wrist feel resting on the plastic? Try describing the way your muscles and tendons move when you type.

Description Two:

There must be rubber sandwiched in there somewhere, somewhere under the brittle plastic keys. The soft, cushioned impact of the key on the board beneath is just too gentle to otherwise explain. My fingers settle down over the shining surface, over the thin film of sebaceous oils left over from my last session, and the session before that, and the session before that. Every once in awhile I look down and admire the natural elegance of my human hand. I watch as the tendons slide frictionless over my knuckles, rippling the skin above and stretching for the shift key. Ten fingers, thirty eight knuckles, two wrists and forty muscles contracting, relaxing in my forearms all working in concert so that I, by tapping on plastic squares, might invade your mind and fill it with my imaginings.

This is better, isn't it? Now let's try a third time, keeping the good things in description two but add in a person. Who is sitting behind the keyboard, hoping to invade your mind? Is he an elderly priest? Perhaps she is a waitress who dreams of becoming an actress. Perhaps the person is none of these things. Look over description three and see how you like it.

Description Three:

I sit down in front of my computer. I am happy, satisfied. The last victim was strong and spirited. I have not felt so invigorated by a murder in years. I feel ***reflective****, perhaps I will think of this keyboard.*

There must be rubber sandwiched in there somewhere, somewhere under the sharp, brittle plastic keys. The cushioned impact of the key on the board beneath is just too gentle to otherwise explain. My fingers settle down over the shining surface, over the thin film of sebaceous oils and bits of gristle left over from my last session, and the session before that, and the session before that. Every once in awhile I look down and admire the natural elegance my powerful, precise human hand. Those same fingers that, just hours before tore fiber from bone, now so delicately tapping. I watch as the tendons slide frictionless over my knuckles, rippling the skin above and stretching for the shift key. Ten fingers, thirty eight knuckles, two wrists and forty muscles contracting, relaxing in my forearms all working in concert so that I, by tapping on this piece of plastic, might reach a thousand kilometers and put this idea straight into your head. I like it there, in your head makes me feel snuggly.

Whatever you think of that last version, I'm betting you aren't bored. Why is the second better than the first? Why is the third better than the second?

The differences between the first description and the second description mostly come down to abstractions and **generalizations** vs. concrete details. An abstraction is a set of rules and generalities taken from several specific things. An abstraction is a concept we cannot touch, see or hear. Love is an abstraction, so is communism, so is truth.

Generalizations are types. "Human" is a generality, for example, since there are billions of humans. "Furniture" is another generality since there are many kinds of furniture. By contrast, concrete details describe a single, particular thing.

Where an abstraction generalizes, concrete details specify. Where a generalization points at a class of things, a concrete detail points at a specific thing. Religious leader is a generalization. Pope Francis is a concrete person. Love is an abstraction. First kiss is a concrete thing.

Caption: The word "boy" is a generalization. The boy on the right is a concrete person.

Generalizations are usually not best in a narrative. For example, think of "the boy." You don't know what this boy looks like, where he lives or what he smells like. "John, the 160 centimeter tall teenage boy with black hair and big, black eyes" is a concrete description. "The boy" could refer to hundreds of millions of people. "John, the 160 centimeter tall teenage boy with black hair and big, black eyes" refers to a particular person. When making a narrative, it is almost always better to use concrete details rather than generalizations.

Abstractions, like generalizations, are not necessarily bad. Indeed, the human ability to abstract is one of the things that makes us uniquely human. Abstractions are necessary to understand concepts like mathematics and language. However, they are much less powerful than concrete details. This is why words like love, freedom and communism are so much more difficult to understand than concrete words like toast, house or hand. We can never touch love, smell freedom or taste communism while we taste toast, smell our hands and touch houses every day. Thus, while abstractions are not bad, they are less real to us than concrete descriptions.

"Jane wants happiness" is an abstract sentence. Jane could mean that she wants a quiet, safe life. It could mean that she wants to watch movies every day or that she wants to paint like Picasso. It could mean that she wants to climb Mt. Everest, we have no way of knowing. "Jane wants a handsome husband,

Concrete representations of happiness, full of concrete details.

to play professional volleyball and take a vacation in Hawaii three times a year" is a concrete way of expressing the same idea as "Jane wants happiness." It is just better because it's much, much more specific and, don't forget, much more interesting.

The reason concrete descriptions are more real goes back to those mirror neurons. When the story-teller talks about "the boy" or "Jane's happiness" it is difficult for the audience's mirror neurons to sync with the storyteller. Maybe the listener is imagining a 3 year-old boy but the storyteller is imagining a 13 year-old boy. Maybe it's so vague the listener gives up and doesn't imagine Jane's happiness at all. However, when the storyteller uses concrete descriptions like height, hair color and age, the listener's mirror neurons can richly imagine "John." The story listener can use his or her mirror neurons to travel inside the storyteller's mind and literally sync brains.

Now that we've explained the difference between the first keyboard description and the second keyboard description, let's work on the differences between the second description and the third. As we discussed in the first chapter, narratives are events and things logically connected. In the second description, we have lots of concrete details of the keyboard, but we don't really connect them to any events. With the introduction of the murderer into description three, we've taken **mere description** and made it into **true narrative**.

True narrative adds movement and change onto descriptions. While human beings are sometimes interested in things that don't change, a beautiful painting, for example life is full of change and most human **endeavor** focuses on understanding, managing and creating changes. You, for example, are taking this class because you want to create a change in your life probably graduating college. Falling in love is about changing from two separate people into a single unit. Buying a designer necklace is about changing the way people see you. There is even research suggesting that people build their personalities by creating a narrative about their lives. There simply isn't very much in life that doesn't change. True narrative is how we explain those changes.

As such, the third keyboard description was best for most people because it combined the concrete details of the second description with events. In other words, true narrative adds action.

To summarize, look at the pictures below. The first shows the quantum uncertainty principle, a pure abstraction - unless you are very good at math - and thus not very fun. The second shows a normal computer keyboard. This is a concrete thing but shows no action. This is better than the quantum uncertainty principle but still not very interesting. The third shows a b-boy performing an "air-flare." This is a concrete thing (concrete dancer, concrete crowd, concrete stage) that is also filled with true narrative action. For most people, it will be far more interesting than the other two pictures.

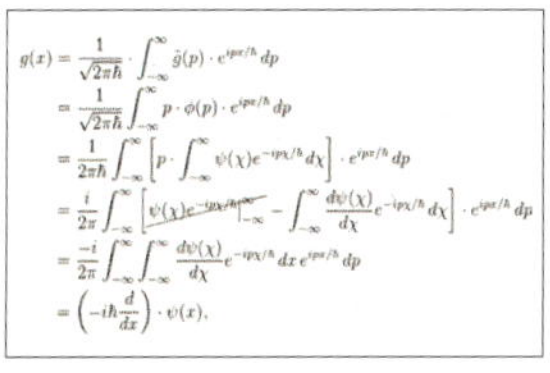

Questions:

Comprehension:

- Of the following phrase pairs, which is more concrete and which is more general/abstract?

"A Plant" or "A Sunflower"	"Bad Pain" or "Broken Finger"	"A Donut" or "A Dessert"
"Ford Mustang" or "Sports Car"	"Water" or "Liquid"	"Shinzo Abe" or "Prime Minister"

Exploration:

- What do you think is easier for students to understand, a very abstract lesson or a very concrete lesson? Explain your reasoning.

____
____
____
____
____
____

- Imagine a popular movie, Batman or Myeongnyang for example. Now remove the true narrative and leave just the setting. How is the movie? Discuss with a classmate.

- Pick an abstract word like success, joy or chemistry and explain it in concrete terms.

RENNS

13

Main Questions	What is the most confusing narrative you've encountered?
	How can leaders make their narratives better?
	What mistakes can make narratives confusing?
	How can you improve engagement with your audience?

Vocabulary	RENNS	Immersive
	Manifestation	Notorious
	Pronoun	Sensation

Now that we've explored the characteristics of good narrative, we should learn how to make good narrative. Unfortunately, making expert narrative is extremely difficult, requiring years of study and practice along with natural talent and excellent observational skills. Very few people have the skill to create a movie like Old Boy, a play like Hamlet or a book like 1Q84. However, there are relatively simple ways to make, if not expert, at least good narratives. A good shortcut is to remember **RENNS**.

This stands for R(easons), E(xamples), N(ames), N(umbers), and S(enses). Filling your narratives with RENNS goes a long ways toward creating clear and interesting stories. Once again, this is not just for writing, RENNS is helpful for any type of narrative.

Reasons

Take a look at the following paragraph and pay close attention. In particular, look for ways it fails as a narrative.

Jane wants to study French Culture at Yale. Vampires always attack the convenience stores. Now her mother would like some cherry ice cream. Nobody likes the smell of garlic.

This paragraph has lots of concrete images. Jane is a specific person, garlic is a specific smell, etc. There are no problematic abstractions. True narrative action is present. Surely this paragraph must be clear and interesting for all readers. Right?

What is the problem? If you remember Ch. 10 in this book, it defines narrative as "anything that logically connects things and events." The paragraph above, for all its good points, fails to logically connect the lovely, concrete things and wonderful, clear events.

If your own narratives don't make sense or aren't logical, it's probably for the same cause the paragraph above failed you don't have enough reasons. When you insert reasons into your narrative, you are basically forcing everything to fit inside the rules of logic.

The easiest way to add reasons to a confusing or illogical narrative is simply to use the words "because" or "so." To demonstrate, let's take the original, nonsense paragraph and rewrite it with "because" and "so."

Jane wants to study French Culture at Yale because the worst vampires come from France. Vampires always attack the convenience stores so she decided to study different convenience foods from France that vampires don't like. Because of her research, she learned that vampires don't like cherry ice cream. Now her mother would like some cherry ice cream so she can keep the local vampires away. Nobody likes the smell of garlic, so cherry ice cream is now the most popular vampire repellent.

Examples of narratives that use reasons very well include J.R.R Tolkien's "Lord of the Rings," Fyodor Dostoyevsky's "Crime and Punishment," and Christopher Nolan's "Interstellar." Because these narratives use reasons very efficiently, they each create realistic, **immersive** experiences for their audiences. Audience members, if they wish, can find many layers of deeper meaning in each of these narratives.

Examples of narratives that fail to be reasonable are "Battlefield Earth," "Southland Tales" and "Film 43." Because nothing in these narratives seems to fit together, audiences were generally confused, bored or frustrated.

Examples

We learned last chapter how abstractions are more difficult for audiences to understand than concrete details. Even simple abstractions like happiness can mean many things to different people. To the first person, happiness might mean money and power. To the second person it might mean quiet and peace. To someone else, it could mean dancing in a nightclub. Complicated abstractions like existentialism, democracy or ennui are even more difficult to understand.

Unfortunately, a narrative that doesn't have any abstractions is likely to be pretty dumb. After all, love, happiness, democracy and race are pretty important ideas even if they are all abstractions. In order to help the audience, good narrative provides examples to show the concrete **manifestations** of abstract ideas. Let's try the difficult abstract idea "concupiscence."

People have to control their concupiscence.

It's very unlikely the audience knows what I mean. First, concupiscence is a very uncommon word and even most native speakers of English won't know what it means. Second, it describes an extremely abstract concept. Third, even if the audience knows what concupiscence means, they have no way to know what specific kind of concupiscence the storyteller has in mind. In situations like this, an example is very useful.

People have to control their concupiscence. For example, no good man would ever steal bread from a beggar just because he wanted a snack. No good woman would kiss a married man in front of his wife just because she felt a little bit lonely. We need to control our destructive desires if we want to be good.

With examples, the audience can figure out what concupiscence means if they don't already know. Further, when used in an example, the storyteller can make the abstract idea of concupiscence - harmful desire - into something concrete and specific.

It's a good idea to use examples whenever you want to describe a difficult, complicated or new idea to the audience. Examples can be written, spoken, acted or expressed in pictures. Regardless of what form, an example serves to give concrete expression to abstract ideas.

Philosophers and scientists often discuss complex and abstract ideas and thus need to use examples efficiently. Niccolo Machiavelli, Brian Greene and Soren Kierkegaard write about extremely complicated ideas but, because they use extensive examples, many people find them enjoyable to read.

On the other hand, Martin Heidegger is **notoriously** impossible to understand and, thus, many fewer people read his work. Many researchers fall into this category, as well. Many academic papers are intentionally confusing because the authors believe this makes them seem more intelligent. These authors are wrong.

Names/Numbers

Using names and numbers instead of **pronouns** and generalizations is a good way to make a narrative more concrete and easier to understand. To see what happens when we use too many pronouns and not enough names, let's look over an example paragraph with all the names removed.

The person went to the place to see the thing. The thing was nicer than the thing from the other place, but not as fun as the person's friend thought it would be. The people decided to go to the other place to see a different thing. Hopefully, it will meet their expectations.

This is awful writing. It's confusing and frustrating to read. It also gives the audience very little information. However, we can easily fix this paragraph simply by replacing the pronouns.

Park Ji-sung went to Paris to see the Louvre. The Louvre was nicer than the 63 Building from Seoul, but not as fun as his friend Monica thought it would be. Monica and Park Ji-sung decided to go to London to see Buckingham Palace. Hopefully, the palace will meet their expectations.

Numbers are similar to names. Vague, uncountable terms like "many, a few, some, etc" make it harder for the audience to clearly understand the storyteller's intent. Let's look at a paragraph that doesn't use numbers.

LeBron James and the Miami Heat beat Kobe Bryant and the Los Angeles Lakers some days ago. Bryant led the Lakers by scoring many points, however, he also missed too many shots. Teammate Pau Gasol had almost as many points but took many fewer shots. LeBron James led the Heat with almost as many points as Bryant, but he took even fewer shots than Gasol. James' teammate Chris Bosh also scored some points and had a few good defensive plays. With the win, the Heat have a lot of wins but only a few losses. The Lakers' record got worse.

This paragraph isn't as bad as the paragraph with no names, and it's true that numbers aren't usually as important as names to a narrative, but this paragraph is still difficult to understand. Let's see what happens when we add numbers.

Lebron James and the Miami Heat beat Kobe Bryant and the Los Angeles Lakers 108-104 three days ago. Bryant led the Lakers by scoring 28 points, however, he also missed 19 of his 30 shots. Teammate Pau Gasol had 23 points with only 7 missed shots out of his 15 attempts. Lebron James led the Heat with 26 points while shooting 11 of 14. James' teammate Chris Bosh also scored 17 points and had at least three excellent defensive plays. With the win, the Heat have 25 wins and only 6 losses. The Lakers fell to 17 wins and 13 losses.

Senses

The last part of RENNS is using **sensation**. This means we should appeal to the audience's five senses when we make narratives. This is because senses are the primary tool people have for learning. Reading requires vision (or touch if you' re blind), learning to ride a bicycle requires touch, vision and hearing. Learning to cook requires taste and smell. As such, our minds are much more efficient when they learn sensually than when they learn through abstractions. Research shows that the more senses a storyteller stimulates the better the audience's engagement[21]. As such, a good storyteller stimulates the audience's eyes, ears, taste buds and noses.

For example, "there was spaghetti and the people ate it" does very little to stimulate the senses. A student or audience member is unlikely to be interested and unlikely to remember anything about the spaghetti later on. However, if we say something like "the kitchen where they made the spaghetti smelled like olive oil and basil. The people eating could feel the hot sauce and taste the tomato juice with each bite," that is much more memorable.

People don't experience a generalized "spaghetti." They feel smooth, starchy noodles with light oil. They see the beautiful bits of basil and black pepper covering the sauce. They smell the fresh bread and hear the wine pouring from the bottle. They taste the sour tomatoes and creamy cheese. As such, if you want your audience to care about spaghetti, you need to talk about the parts of spaghetti they actually experience.

21 Narrative vs. Abstract http://www.stevedenning.com/Business-Narrative/narrative-vs-abstract-thinking-Bruner.aspx

Examples of storytellers who are very good at senses include novelists Jane Austen, Mohsin Hamid and Margaret Atwood, along with poets John Donne and Dante Alighieri. Any movie or play will almost automatically be filled with sense images.

Examples of things that generally fail to include senses are legal documents, accounting documents, bad textbooks and many academic papers. In other words, most boring narratives lack sense details.

Questions

Comprehension:

- What is RENNS?

Exploration:

- Find the problem with each sentence and fix it.

The girl went to the place.

____

____

Jane ate some pizzas at a few parties.

____

____

I hate onions. John has seven friends in Egypt.

____

____

Activity:

- Use an example to explain one of the following abstract concepts. Freedom. Hatred. Religion. Contentment. Capitalism.

____

____

- Appeal to the audience's senses while describing one of the following things: Music. A couch. Korean food. The ocean. Baseball.

____

____

Project:

- After each part of RENNS, there were examples of good and bad narratives. Choose one of the following good examples -

JRR Tolkien's "Lord of the Rings," Fyodor Dostoyevski's "Crime and Punishment," Christopher Nolan's "Interstellar," Brian Greene's "Fabric of the Cosmos," Soren Kierkegaard's "Fear and Trembling," Jane Austen's "Pride and Prejudice," Mohsin Hamid's "A Beheading," Margaret Atwood's "The Handmaid's Tale," Dylan Thomas' "Do Not Go Gentle into That Good Night," or Dante Alighieri's "Inferno."

After you have read or watched a good example, compare it with a bad example-

Roger Christian's "Battlefield Earth," Richard Kelly's "Southland Tales," Peter Farrelly's "Film 43," Martin Heidegger's "Being and Time" or the American IRS' "1040a Tax Form."

- Rewrite your story from Ch. 10 using what you learned about narrative. Present your changes and explain why you made those changes.

14 What Is Informal Logic?

Main Questions	What are the differences between logical and illogical statements?
	What are your rules for understanding a story?
	How can logic help students recognize deception or sloppy thinking?
	How can logic help leaders plan for the future?

Vocabulary	Logic	Completeness
	Validity	Informal Logic
	Consistency	Naturalistic Fallacy
	Soundness	Deduction

All **logic** is an attempt to systematically understand arguments. Among the dozens of types of logic that demonstrate argument **validity**, we will focus most on informal and deductive logic. This is because logic is important for understanding why arguments succeed or fail.

If we try to make the argument that "2+2 = potato," for example, most people will immediately feel that it is not a logical argument. However, we need to explain why "2+2= potato" is not logical if we really want to understand. Do you know why "2+2= potato" is illogical?

All logical systems need three things - **consistency**[22], **soundness**[23], and **completeness**[24]. Thus, when we look over the symbolic logical system "2+2 = potato," we can reject it because "potato" is not consistent with "2+2," it is not sound because we would normally conclude "2+2 = 4" and it is not complete because we cannot offer proof that "2+2 = potato."

However, logic does not just apply to symbols or mathematics. Inductive logic uses these rules to start with evidence and create a theory. Informal logic, which is what we will be primarily studying, applies the principles of consistency, soundness and completeness to normal sentences. Deductive logic, which we will also study, starts with theories and determines specific results.

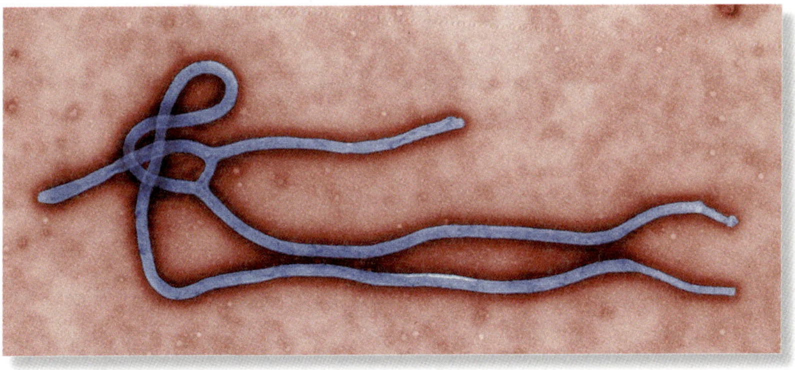

The Ebola virus is natural. Doesn't that mean it's also good? (Source CDC)

22 There are no contradictions.

23 All answers in the the system will always be true.

24 Any answer in the system can be proven.

Informal Logic

Let's look at an example of **informal logic**[25] in action. Consider the argument that "the Ebola virus is natural and therefore Ebola is good." Most people would certainly disagree with the conclusion, but without informal logic, it is difficult to explain why the argument is wrong. However, if you are good at informal logic, you can recognize the argument contains a **naturalistic fallacy**[26]. This means that, in a logical argument, you cannot assume that nature is automatically moral or good. The "ebola is good" argument is only valid if you assume all natural things are good, which is simply false. "Good and bad" are a separate and unrelated category from "natural and unnatural."

Narrative makes people listen. Logic makes narrative valid.
Narrative without logic is empty. Logic without narrative is boring.
You need both!

It's important that future leaders like you learn logic, especially now that you know how to create narratives. The reason is that your ability to create good narratives keeps your followers interested. They will listen to you. If you don' t understand logic, you are very likely to teach those people stupid or unrealistic things in your class.

Informal logic is the logic of newspaper articles, advertising, and legal codes. It is the logic of ethics. It is the logic of movies and pop songs. It is the tool by which we analyze our opinions and the opinions of others. Most important, it is the type of logic most effectively applied to leadership.

Since informal logic is so important to our everyday lives, we need to know the differences between good and bad arguments. In order to understand good and bad arguments, we need to understand deduction, paradox and especially fallacies. Fallacies are so important, in fact, that the next chapter will discuss nothing but fallacies.

25 A type of logic that focuses on the way people talk.

26 A logical problem caused by people confusing the meaning of "natural" with the meaning of "good."

Caption: These are examples of everyday speech. Informal logic is the best tool for finding the validity of these advertisements and slogans.

Deduction

Deduction is a way of going from a premise (beginning assumption) to necessary conclusions. This means that, in deduction, if the premises are true and the meaning of each word is true then the conclusion must also be true. Let's try an example of deduction.

(Premise 1) All airplanes are machines.

(Premise 2) All machines break eventually.

(Necessary Conclusion) All airplanes break eventually.

With deduction, we can attack the premises. We might say that an airplane is not really a machine or that not all machines break. If we accept the premises, though, the only possible conclusion is that airplanes eventually break.

It's impossible for any of the premises to be true while the conclusion is false in a valid, deductive argument.

However, we need to be careful with deductive logic because it's easy to create invalid deductive systems. For example, let's look at the failed deductive system below.

All men have beards?

(Premise 1) John has a beard.

(Premise 2) John is a man.

(Conclusion) All men have beards.

Why is this deduction invalid? Experience is the most obvious answer. We see men without beards all the time. However, there is also a logical problem. The definition of "man" does not include "has a beard." Therefore, we cannot conclude that just because John has a beard, all men have beards. As such, it's important that when we make deductive arguments or analyze deductive arguments, we are very careful with the definitions of our premises and conclusions.

Paradox

A **paradox** is a type of argument that cannot be true. Paradoxes come in two basic types and point to problems in arguments. When a seemingly logical argument ends in paradox (which they often do), it is a sign there is a problem in the argument or that the problem needs more investigation.

The first type of paradox is **contradiction**. "I went up-down." Going up is a direct contradiction with going down. If an argument requires you to go up-down, there is an error somewhere in the premises, definitions or process of building an argument. Another example is the following: “This sentence is untrue.” If the sentence is true, then it is untrue. If the sentence is untrue, then it is true. The result is nonsense.

The second type of paradox is called “infinite regress.” This is pretty complicated and not a common problem for most people, but we should understand it at least on a surface level. A good example is standing between two mirrors. If you look into the mirror, you will see a mirror within a mirror within a mirror within a mirror on into infinity. This is an infinite regression paradox because every conclusion requires more explanation. A mirror is inside the mirror which is inside the mirror which is inside the mirror which is inside the mirror etc.

The pictures above are visual examples of the infinite regression paradox. This type of paradox is possible in normal language, but it’s not very common. Here’s an example.

John: *The world is flat and rests on a turtle’s back.*

Jane: *What is under the turtle?*

John: *Another turtle.*

Jane: *And what is under that turtle?*

John: *Another turtle.*

Jane: *How many turtles are there?*

John: *It’s turtles all the way down.*

Questions:

Comprehension:

- What is deductive logic?
- What is a paradox?
- How are premises and conclusions related in a deductive system?

Practice:

- Find the premises and conclusions in these deductive arguments.

(A) Drinking whiskey adds excitement and sophistication to your life. Excitement and sophistication are very desirable for all people. Therefore, you should drink whiskey.

(B) We should use human feces as fertilizer for crops. This is because human feces is a good, natural fertilizer. Also, it's wrong to waste resources and human feces is a good resource.

(C) Exporting K-pop to other Asian countries spreads the power of Korean culture. We should export K-pop to as many countries as possible. When we spread Korean culture it creates opportunities for Korean citizens.

- Go back to those three deductive arguments, choose one and attack the premises.

____

____

____

____

____

____

____

____

____

____

Exploration:

- Look up the "Missing Dollar Paradox," "The Barber Paradox," "The Omnipotence Paradox," "The Arrow Paradox," "Achilles and the Tortoise Paradox," "The Unexpected Hanging Paradox" and "The Liar's Paradox." Explain one of them to your classmates. (You can use Korean)

- Some paradoxes are eventually solved. Find an example.

15 Fallacies

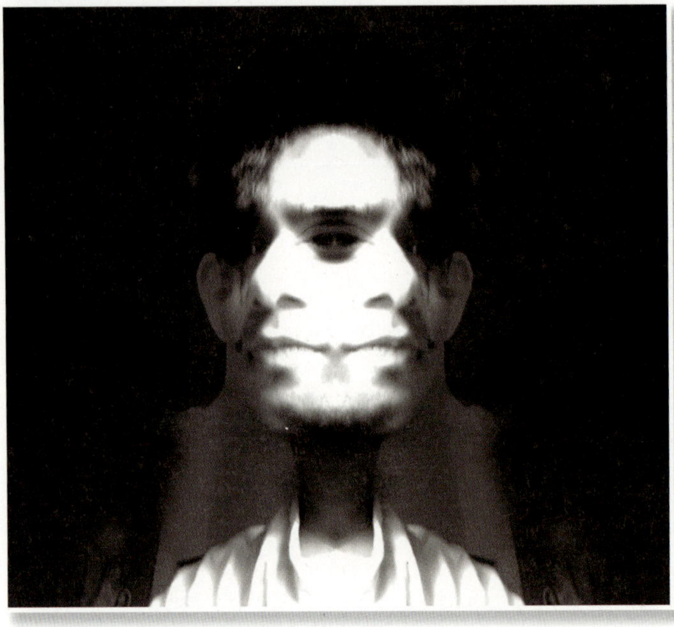

Main Questions	Do you think politicians and advertisers use proper logic?
	How do malicious people use fallacies to deceive others?
	What fallacies are leaders most vulnerable to?
	What fallacies are followers most vulnerable to?

Vocabulary	Malicious	Fraud
	Self-Deception	Conspiracy Theory
	Demagogue	Factor

As we saw in the previous chapter, deductive systems can fail because of false premises, incorrect definitions or paradoxes. Fallacies are, at their base, specific ways to fail in a logical system. There are an infinite number of potential fallacies, but the important fallacies are ones that seem true. These true-seeming fallacies, when used **maliciously**, are tools for deception or **fraud**. Many advertisements are intentionally deceptive fallacies of this sort, as are many forms of political speech. When used unintentionally, fallacies become tools for **self-deception** or ignorance. Most **conspiracy theories**, which can be very dangerous when many people believe them, are forms of unintentionally fallacious thinking. As leaders, then, it is our duty to understand and avoid fallacies as much as possible.

Therefore, in this chapter we will explore some of the most common and dangerous fallacies. As you read try to think of examples of each fallacy in your normal life.

Middle Ground Fallacy/Appeal to Moderation

This fallacy makes the incorrect assumption that the middle course is always best. For example, imagine your friend is accused of robbery. The prosecutor wants your friend to go to jail for ten years. Your friend says "I'm innocent and shouldn't go to jail at all." A middle ground would be to just send your friend to jail for five years because it' s 'moderate.' Another example is driving. If you look at the photo below, you can clearly see the driver is being dangerous.

Caption: This driver is avoiding the extreme right and extreme left sides of the road, so she is being safe, right?

However, if we use the middle ground fallacy, we need to say "driving on the left side of the road is 'extreme' and so is driving on the right side. Therefore, you should drive your car in the middle of the road."

The middle ground fallacy is invalid because it misuses the definition of the words "moderate" and "extreme." While moderation is often good, it is in a separate category from good or bad. While extremes are often bad, extreme is not in the category of good or bad. It is good to be an extremely skilled dentist, for example, while it is bad to be a moderate bank robber.

Appeal to Nature/Naturalistic Fallacy

This argument confuses the meaning of natural with the meanings of good and bad. More fundamentally, this fallacy assumes that things *as they are is* the same as *things as they should be*. This fallacy is common in fields as diverse as religion, science, medicine and philosophy. *You should buy X Brand milk because it's 100% natural, or, antibiotics are unnatural and therefore it is wrong to take medicine*, for example.

Caption: These three Mormon Crickets are eating a fourth cricket. So cannibalism is natural and therefore good?

Genetic Fallacy

This is a dishonest sort of argument. It ignores the substance of an argument and focuses instead on the argument's origin. This fallacy is extremely common among moralists, **demagogues** and the self-righteous in general. Take the following example:

John: *I think that we should care for the poor.*
Jane: *You know that Otto Von Bismark, an immoral man, invented the welfare state, right?*
Or ~
Jane: *I like sugar.*
John: *Slavery is the only reason sugar farming got started!*

Caption: Hitler and Stalin both liked art. That doesn't mean liking art makes you a dangerous dictator.

This fallacy is invalid because the origin of the argument has no relationship with the validity of the argument. Just because sugar farming began because of slavery does not make candy wrong. Just because a good person invented dolls does not mean you must like playing with dolls. The origin of an argument has no necessary relationship with the truth of an argument.

Ad Hominem

This is closely related to the genetic fallacy. Instead of focusing on the origin of the argument, the ad hominem fallacy focuses on the person making the argument. The characteristics of the person making the argument is not a valid reason for accepting or rejecting an argument. Ad hominem is a dishonest attempt to distract from the argument.

John: *I think we should continue to explore space.*
Jane: *That's because you're fat and stupid.*

Even if John is fat and stupid, that does not mean we should stop space exploration. There is no necessary relationship between John's personality or body shape and exploring space.

Appeal to Authority

This is essentially ad hominem in reverse. In this case, the fallacy says you must believe something because an authority figure made the argument. Just like ad hominem, it fails because authority figures can be wrong. "*If Kim-gu said it, it must be true.*"

Moving the Goalposts/No True Scotsman

This is a fairly common fallacy for people who want to protect their beliefs. Basically, this is the practice of changing definitions or standards whenever your opponent finds a mistake in your reasoning.

John: *You are a murderer and have to go to prison.*
Jane: *But I shouldn't go to prison. There's no reason I have to go to prison.*
John: *But if we don't punish murderers there will be chaos. You are a murderer and so we have to punish you.*
Jane: *That's true about chaos, but I wouldn't like prison. I shouldn't have to go.*

In this example, Jane invents a new standard for punishing murders - “I wouldn’t like it” - when her original argument - “there’s no reason I have to go to prison” - fails.

A variation on moving the goalposts is called the No True Scotsman fallacy. This is simply changing definitions so that your argument can never be wrong. For example:

John: *No Scotsman is a coward.*
Jane: *Mary, who is a Scotsman, always runs away from danger. She is a coward.*
John: *No TRUE Scotsman is a coward.*

John has just changed the definition of true Scotsman to mean “Scotsmen who are not cowards.” As such, John’s argument that true Scotsmen are never cowards becomes meaningless. Effectively, John said

“Scotsmen who are not cowards are not cowards.”

Straw Man Fallacy

This fallacy distorts an opponent’s arguments by making the argument ridiculous. If Jane uses a straw man, she is no longer really discussing the original argument and, therefore, her conclusions are invalid. Once again, this is very common in political speech, amongst conspiracy theorists and in internet discussion boards. For example:

John: *I want to bring more chocolate to our city because I think chocolate makes people happy.*

These are literal straw men. In an argument, making a fake, extreme version of your opponent’s argument is called “strawmanning.”

Jane: *You want to build our streets and homes out of chocolate instead of metal and concrete! (Extreme and ridiculous version of John's argument.) That's a horrible idea! (Invalid conclusion.)*

Slippery Slope Fallacy

This is an assumption that doing (*X*) will inevitably lead to an extreme version of (*X*). This is a fallacy because the definition of (*X*) does not include "the most extreme version of (*X*)." This can overlap with strawmanning. For example:

Jane: *I think we should encourage businesses to come to our city.*
John: *If we encourage businesses they will inevitably destroy our government and make everyone into a corporate slave!*

The definition of business does not include "destroys the government" or "makes everyone into a corporate slave." Thus, the argument is invalid.

Appeal to Ignorance/Appeal to Fear

This is fallacy is most commonly used by authority figures to justify action to their followers. The basic assumption is "we don't know what (*X*) means, so therefore we should do what I believe," or, alternately "(*X*) is scary so we should just do what I believe." This is a fallacy because "we don't know" does not imply that a certain thing is true or untrue and "it's scary" doesn't imply "I'm right." For example:

John: *We don't know what's causing the economic recession. It's so confusing and scary.*
Jane: *I agree. It's very mysterious and frightening. That's why we need to be very strict in following my economic plan.*

Non-Sequitur

This is a type of argument that fails because it attempts to draw connections between unrelated things. Non sequiturs are probably the easiest kind of fallacy to spot but can sometimes be hidden very well in deceptive arguments. Here is an easy example:

Studying Chinese is good because cake is delicious.

Studying Chinese and the taste of cake simply are not related. The argument makes no connection between the Chinese language and cake and is thus nonsense. However, non-sequiturs also have harder to spot varieties like this one:

The Korean economy improved during Sejong the Great's time as king. Therefore, King Sejong was a good economic leader.

This is making the false assumption that King Sejong is the only possible cause of the good economy. He could be the cause, but the argument presents no evidence that the growth wasn't caused by trade with China, successful wars, scientific advances or some combination of other **factors**.
Now that we have a good understanding of most common logical fallacies, we have one more to deal with. I left it for last because it is really important to understand the difference between validity and correctness.

The Fallacy Fallacy

The fallacy fallacy says that because an argument is fallacious, its conclusion is automatically wrong. It makes the assumption that invalid logic always leads to wrong conclusions, which simply isn't true. Invalid arguments can be true. Let's take a look at this ridiculous, fallacious but ultimately correct argument.

The sky is blue. This is true because my mother said so. It is also true because cucumbers grow on the moon and anybody who disagrees with me is just jealous and ugly. It is true because if we don't believe the sky is blue then aliens will steal our babies. Since the other reasons are so complicated, everyone should just believe me that the sky is blue.

This argument is absolute garbage. It contains an appeal to authority, a non-sequitur, false premises, ad hominem, an appeal to fear and an appeal to ignorance. However, its conclusion is still true. The sky really is blue. This leads to an uncomfortable question then. If we can be correct with bad logic, why do we need logic?

The answer is that any correct conclusion will have a logically valid explanation, even if we don't know what it is yet. For example, the sky's blueness has a logically valid explanation - gasses in the atmosphere absorb different colors of light, leaving blue to reach our eyes. Further, in a logically valid but incorrect argument, the systematic nature of logical arguments allows you to learn from your mistakes.

If you have a logically valid argument that the world is flat, for example, you can easily learn why the world is not flat when given new evidence (ie, corrected premises). If your reasons for believing the world is flat are illogical, that illogical system will not help you learn when you get new evidence.

Further, while logically invalid arguments *can* be true, they usually aren't. A logically invalid argument has an essentially random relationship with truth. Logically valid arguments have a much higher chance of being true because they have a better than random relationship with truth.

Questions:

Comprehension:

- What is a fallacy?
- What is the ad hominem fallacy?
- What is the slippery slope fallacy?
- What is the appeal to ignorance fallacy?

Exploration:

- What sorts of fallacies do you find most often in advertisements? Find a specific example and analyze it.

  ____

  ____

  ____

  ____

- Politicians often use fallacies in their speeches. What fallacies can you find examples of?

Group Activity:

- The fallacy fallacy says that just because an argument is invalid does not mean that the conclusion is wrong. Why is logic important if invalid arguments can be true? Discuss with classmates.
- What fallacy do you think is most dangerous? Present your findings to the class as a whole.

16 Cognitive Biases and Distortions

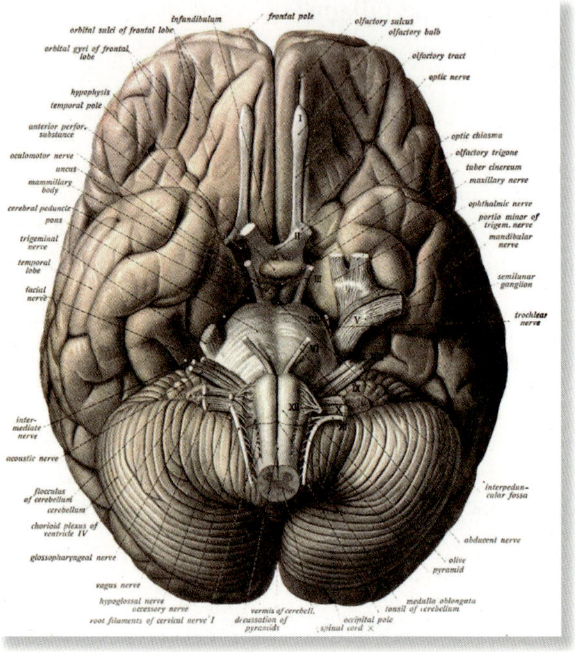

Main Questions	
	What are some natural weaknesses in your thinking?
	Are most people harsher with others or themselves?
	When was the last time you listened to a politician or religious leader you disagree with?
	Why are people more afraid of kidnappers than bathtubs?

Vocabulary		
	Fundamental Attribution Error	Bias
	Confirmation Bias	Empiricism
	Probability	Negativity

We should understand just how powerful our minds are. According to Martin Hilbert and Priscila Lopez's paper in Science Magazine, the entire computation power of all the world's computers in 2007, 6.4X10^18 instructions per second, is roughly equal to the maximum processing power of a single human brain. The total data stored in the world's computers in 2007, Hilbert and Lopez said, is roughly equal to the amount of data stored in a single person's DNA.

Think about what that means. The grey stuff between your ears is roughly as powerful as every X-Box, home PC, super computer, calculator and smartphone in the world in 2007, *combined*. You are incredibly powerful. If some mad scientist tried to upload the all of information stored in just your body's DNA he would overwhelm and crash *the entire internet*. According to "The Independent" the fourth most powerful computer in the world, using enough electricity to power several houses, needed 40 minutes to simulate one percent of a human brain operating for *one second*.

Now that we know how logic fails (fallacies), we should next focus on the reasons why logic fails. Obviously, there are millions of potential reasons, but some of the most important come from natural weaknesses in the ways our minds work. Fortunately, if we recognize these weaknesses, we can use our incredibly powerful brains to correct these weaknesses and become more logical.

This is a part of the computer that simulated 1% of a brain thinking for 1 second. It needed almost an hour to complete the job.

Fundamental Attribution Error

Fundamental attribution error in action.

I recently walked into a public restroom as another man was walking out. As I approached my stall, the lights turned off and I immediately blamed the other man for being rude. Didn't he see me enter the bathroom? Couldn't he realize I would need the light? I said "what a jerk" and got irritated.

Then, when I walked out of the restroom I noticed something on the wall. There was a sensor that automatically turned the lights off and on. The man, the "jerk," hadn't done anything rude at all. He probably didn't even notice the lights turning off and, even if he did, he couldn't control that sensor. I had unfairly blamed that man for something he could not possibly be at fault for.

Why? Am I just an angry, unreasonable person? I hope not, but even if I am, that's probably not why I was unfair. It is much more likely I was fooled by my own **fundamental attribution error**[27].

This **bias** is present in almost all people. It is a tendency to overemphasize the importance of people's personalities and ignore their circumstances. For example:

John: *The boxer didn't lose the fight because his knee is injured, he lost because he's a weak and cowardly person.*

Jane: *The economy didn't get better because of long term investment trends or better educated workers, it got better because of the president's personal guidance.*

Mary: *The student didn't forget his homework because he had too many tests and got tired, he forgot his homework because he's irresponsible and lazy.*

With the fundamental attribution error, it is useful to remember that context matters. Indeed, in many cases, context matters more than the personalities of the people involved.

27 Blaming problems on personalities and ignoring circumstance.

If you prefer an amusing quotation, Napoleon Bonaparte has you covered:

"Never ascribe to malice that which is adequately explained by incompetence."

Confirmation Bias

Most people like to hear things they already agree with. Communists love to talk about how unfair capitalism is. Atheists feel great when they hear a story about how god/God/gods don't exist.

Isn't it nice when you can listen to things you already believe?

Now, imagine the communists discovered evidence that communism was unfair and atheists learned that atheism was logically problematic. How angry will these people be? How likely are they to listen to the new evidence?

Because of **confirmation bias**, they are almost certain to ignore evidence that doesn't agree with their preexisting beliefs. This bias causes people to ignore huge amounts of evidence. Let me give you some possible examples of confirmation bias.

Atheists generally have no idea what the cosmological argument means, if they even know what it is (which they usually don't). They don't often understand the unprovable assumptions of **empiricism**.[28] Religious people very often counter atheists by not understanding how evolution works, appealing to ignorance and ignoring the problem of evil.[29]

Many people find it infuriating to listen to groups like these. The more confirmation bias there is, the more likely that the people arguing are both very confident and very ignorant - a perfect recipe for annoying everyone else.

The more strongly people believe in something[30], the more likely you are to be blinded by confirmation bias. This is why discussions about sensitive subjects - patriotic things, religion, race - are often so mind-numbingly stupid.

However, we don't have to surrender to confirmation bias and idiocy. Giles Fraser, and English Christian priest, has written some of the best pro-Christian articles[31] I've ever seen and he was able to do so because he is deeply, intimately familiar with the opponents of Christianity - Marx and Nietzsche in this case. If you want to be more like Giles Fraser and less like the crazy uncle who ruins family gatherings, you should overcome confirmation bias as much as possible. In other words, it is more important to understand a thing than to believe a thing.

---

28 Basically, the cosmological argument says that cause and effect must have broken down at some point in the past. Without cause and effect, empiricism (science) is nonsense. Visit http://bengarrido.com/you-dont-know-jack/ for more information.

29 The problem of evil says that God cannot exist if there is evil in the universe. For more information visit http://plato.stanford.edu/entries/evil/.

30 Cotton, J. L. (1985). Cognitive dissonance in selective exposure. In D. Zillmann & J. Bryant (Eds.), Selective exposure to communication (pp. 11-33). Hillsdale, NJ: Erlbaum.

31 Fraser was raised as a communist and his exploration of Nietzschean atheism led him to convert to Christianity. https://www.theguardian.com/commentisfree/2012/feb/05/passionate-atheism-me-christianity-nietzsche or https://www.theguardian.com/commentisfree/belief/2008/nov/24/philosophy-religion-nietzsche-girard

Probability Biases

Human beings are generally pretty bad at estimating **probabilities**. For example, lots of people are afraid of murderers and terrorists but very few people are afraid of stairs or taxi cabs. This is odd, since you are much more likely to die falling down the stairs than being killed by a murderer and a taxi crash is much more likely to harm you than a terrorist attack.

Probability biases also show up in gambling. Most people, after losing at poker seven times in a row, behave as if they have better chances on the eighth attempt. This is because the gambler doesn't understand that each hand of poker is an independent event. Casino owners, obviously, like it when gamblers suffer from this bias.

Negativity bias is another probability bias. People are naturally more likely to pay attention to bad news than good news. This is probably a good thing in most situations. For example, it is more important to pay attention to bad news - a tiger is getting ready to attack - than good news - these flowers are beautiful. However, if we aren't aware of this bias, it can lead to faulty premises. For example, most Americans believe that violence and crime are getting worse even though this is the exact opposite of the truth.[32]

There are other types of cognitive bias, but the three listed above are common in educational and workplace environments. Unless you, future leaders, understand them and prepare, it will be difficult to think clearly.

And that, clear thinking, is the entire point of this book. It is my sincere hope that with narrative, you learned to express your ideas clearly and enjoyably. With informal logic, I hope you learned how to make your ideas worthy of expression.

32 Crime and fear of crime. http://reason.com/blog/2014/10/23/crime-fears-clown-fears

Questions:

Comprehension:

- What is the fundamental attribution error?
- Why do people have negativity bias?
- How does confirmation bias affect discussions?

Exploration:

- What cognitive biases are most difficult for you? Why do you think they are difficult?
- Which cognitive biases do you think are most closely connected with the genetic fallacy, the slippery slope fallacy or the no true Scotsman fallacy? Explain your reasoning.

____

____

____

____

____

Activity:

- Choose your most strongly held belief. Think about it deeply and decide whether confirmation bias distorts your view of this belief.

How Leaders and Followers Relate

17

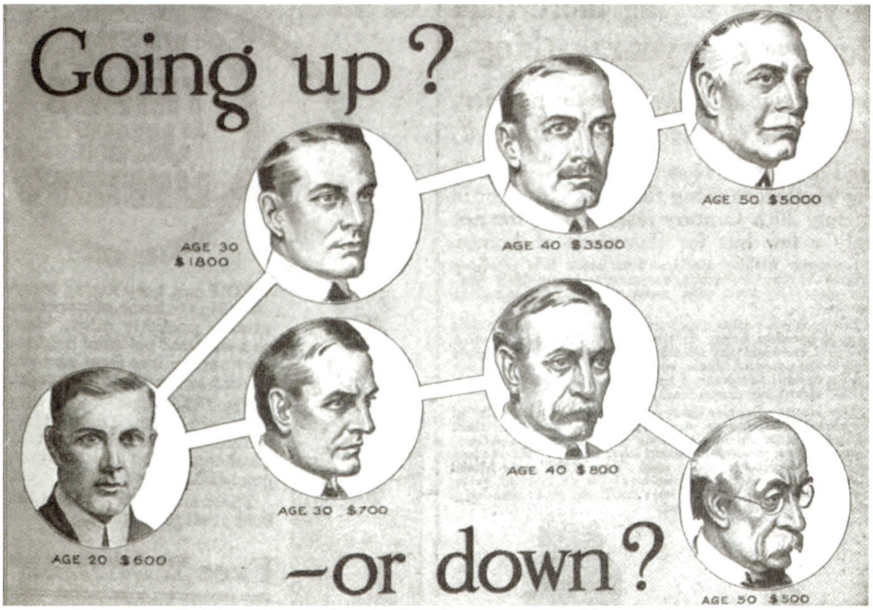

Main Questions	Are people naturally good or bad?
	How well can leaders predict their students' or workers' futures?
	How moral are good people?
	How immoral are bad people?
	How important are environmental factors for people's behavior?

Vocabulary	Essentialist	Implications	Benign
	Delousing	Solitary Confinement	Dissociate
	Anonymous		

Now that you realize how important your job is, it's important to start making a strategy for dealing with your followers. One of the first things you must decide is if your quiet student is naturally quiet, your bad workers are naturally bad and your good followers are naturally good. If you believe that your followers are naturally good/bad/quiet, you are an **essentialist**.

Goodness

Are people naturally good or bad? Is the evil of Kim Gil-tae, for example, just a natural part of his psychology? Was Eom Hong-gil born brave? Perhaps Yoo Jae-seok would always be a funny, kind man, regardless of his circumstances.

This is an incredibly important question for leaders to answer. From the first minute a teacher steps into the classroom, they will have smart kids, dumb kids, good kids, bad kids and noisy kids. From the first minute a public official begins working, they will deal with reasonable citizens and unreasonable citizens, people who care about the community and people who are selfish. If these citizens and students are naturally smart, dumb, good, bad or noisy, selfish or unselfish, your leadership is relatively unimportant.

Sure, you can protect the unselfish citizens from the selfish citizens. You can punish the noisy kids to control their natural tendency to disrupt class, perhaps, but you can't really change them. With the naturally dumb people, really the best thing you can do is help them accept their inferiority. With the naturally bad people, I don't even know what you can do.

This is a very depressing way to look at people, but if we're essentialists it's really the only honest thing we can do. Indeed, many professionals believe in essentialism. They are being essentialist whenever they say something like "I give up on you," "you're just a bad person," "you're just a punk" or "you're just a typical (whatever) and you'll never change." However, they are also being essentialist when they tell good students things like "you are so pretty, you will be fine," "you're just a good person," or "you are so smart."

Essentialism also has uncomfortable **implications** for smart people and good people. If a person is naturally smart, for example, they really don't need to work hard. After all, they will naturally succeed because they will always be smart. Why do naturally good workers need guidance if morality is just a part of their personalities?

The benefit of essentialism is that it is very easy to understand. If all students are naturally good/bad/whatever, then teachers have a convenient way to understand their classes. If all workers are naturally smart or stupid, a manager doesn't need to think very much at all. Further, essentialism is a handy way for leaders to avoid stress. After all, poor or challenging students often fail. Dumb workers often can't do their work. If we are essentialist teachers, we don't have to feel bad when our students get worse. If we are essentialist managers, we don't have to care when our dumb workers spiral into disaster.

However, we need to decide if essentialism is a valid explanation for human behavior. To investigate this, we should look at the Stanford Prison Experiment.[33]

The Stanford Prison Experiment

Dr. Philip Zimbardo, a psychology professor at Stanford University, wanted to know what was more important to a person's behavior, their essential personality or their environments. In 1971, in order to find out, he organized a simulated prison at Stanford University's Psychology Department.

In order to make sure there were no naturally bad people, he carefully chose 24 male Stanford undergraduate students. None used drugs, none had ever been convicted of a crime, none had mental illnesses. Zimbardo excluded any applicant with patterns of odd or unconventional behavior. They were, in other words, as normal and average as possible.

Zimbardo then randomly divided the 24 students into two groups. Twelve became "prison guards." The other twelve became "prisoners." It's very important you remember this was random. The only difference between a guard and a prisoner, at the beginning of the experiment, was pure, random chance.

33 https://prezi.com/nvqtj7latm0b/the-stanford-prison-experiment/

Zimbardo built the experiment this way because he wanted to test these essentialist assumptions. If essential personalities were the most important things, then the prisoners and guards would not change their behaviors from their natural, **benign** personalities. They would remain kind, normal college boys. However, if the environment was more important than the students' essential personalities, then we would expect the boys' behavior to change when they became guards or prisoners.

In order to change the environment for the prisoner-students, Zimbardo had the prisoner students arrested by real policemen. (The policemen had volunteered to help in the experiment.) Next, the policemen took the prisoners' fingerprints and put them inside the fake prison at Stanford University. At the fake prison, the student guards stripped the prisoners naked and **deloused** them. After this, the guards gave the prisoners embarrassing, skirt-like prison clothes and changed their names into numbers. Zimbardo believed that these things would make the students feel like real prisoners - powerless, dehumanized and humiliated.

Soldier being cleaned and prepared for delousing.

In order to change the environment for the guard-students, Zimbardo gave them large sunglasses, police batons and uniforms. Zimbardo believed each of these things would give the student-guards a particular feeling. He believed that the glasses would act like masks, hiding the guard's identity. He believed that the batons would be symbols of power and that the clothes would make the guards feel like important officials. He told the guards to "control" the prisoners and "act like the boss" but gave almost no specific instructions.

Zimbardo wanted to make the experiment feel realistic, but all the boys knew that the prison was fake, the "criminals" were not really criminals and that the "guards" were not really guards. Zimbardo told all the boys that they could quit the experiment at any time, for any reason.

For the first couple of hours, the students mostly act awkward. However, when the guards give some simple orders the prisoners refuse to obey. From this point on, the student's behavior becomes much more brutal.

Before the end of the first day, guards force prisoners to wake up at 2:30 AM and do difficult exercises. On the second day, the prisoners have a riot and insult the guards. The guards respond by shooting the prisoners with fire extinguishers. When the prisoners finally give up, the guards take away the prisoners' beds, make them strip naked and take the prisoner leaders to **solitary confinement**. They also force prisoners to defecate and urinate into buckets inside the prison cells. The feces and urine would not be cleaned and remained with the prisoners.

After only 36 hours, Prisoner 8612 suffers an emotional breakdown. Zimbardo sends him home before he suffers permanent mental damage. From day three the guards, still feeling threatened by the prisoners, limit the prisoners to a few hours of sleep per night. Two or three times a night, the guards wake all the prisoners up and make them do exercises, clean toilets with their hands or sing songs.

At the beginning of the fourth day, Prisoner 819 can't stop crying. The prisoners, instead of helping the boy, cooperate with the guards to further embarrass and mock Prisoner 819. Guards began physically abusing prisoners.

On the fifth day, Prisoner 1037 becomes so depressed he almost can't move. Prisoner 416 refuses to eat, planning to starve himself. The guards lock Prisoner 416 into solitary confinement. Later that day, guards force prisoners to hug and say "I love you" to other prisoners. Sleep deprivation becomes even more extreme. On the sixth day, Zimbardo cancels the experiment.

Analysis

The Stanford Prison Experiment raises a lot of questions. Why did the guards become so brutal? What were the reasons the fake prison became so terrible? What were the mechanisms that made the prisoners into animals?

It's important to remember that any of the students could have quit at any time. None of them did. All of the prisoners who left the experiment were removed by Zimbardo. Nobody asked to leave. They betrayed each other continuously through the experiment and helped the guards torment weaker prisoners. The prisoners chose to starve, have emotional breakdowns and endure torture rather than quit the experiment. They even lied to their parents rather than admit how miserable their situations had become.

None of the guards asked to leave. Several of the guards felt that abusing the prisoners was wrong, but none of them complained or tried to stop the abuses. None of them asked to quit the experiment. None of them challenged Dr. Zimbardo or the more aggressive guards. When the experiment ended, all the guards felt disappointed. They were just beginning to get good at being guards. It was not until the experiment ended and the students put their normal clothes back on that they expressed any guilt. Once back in their normal environments, most of the guards did feel very guilty.

What happened? If we use our essentialist beliefs, we will say things like "the guards were terrible people. I can't believe how cruel they were." Maybe we will shake our heads and explain that the prisoners must have been terrible people to act like such animals.

This is a morally comfortable way to think. It is simple. We can understand an essentialist belief like this without thinking too hard. More importantly, it allows us to see the world as a simple contest between heroes and villains. It allows us to avoid thinking and avoid responsibility.

However, an essentialist would have a very hard time explaining why all 24 college boys hadn't done anything animal-like or brutal before the experiment began. It would seem ridiculous to assume that all 12 of the boys randomly chosen to be guards were the exact same 12 who were secretly brutal all along. It seems incredibly unlikely that a perfect collection of 12 "hidden animals" would just happen to perfectly match the 12 prisoners in the experiment. It seems ridiculous to believe that all 24 hidden psychos would choose to reveal their true personalities in the same six-day period.

A cynical essentialist who believes that most people are essentially evil can't really explain the experiment either. After all, if people are essentially evil, why hadn't these college boys done evil things before the experiment?

According to Dr. Zimbardo and other psychologists, the only three things the experiment really required were new clothes, a bad or weak boss and a new location.

For new clothes, the prisoners' embarrassing skirts and frequent nakedness made them feel and look like animals. On the other hand, the guard's sunglasses hid their faces and identities. This made it easier for guards and prisoners to **dissociate** from their normal identities as friendly, regular college students.

This is a powerful effect. Studies have found that Native American tribes that used war paint to hide their identities, for example, were much more likely to torture prisoners than tribesmen who did not cover their faces. Further, the New Yorker Magazine[34] found that **anonymous** internet commenters, who also hide their identities, were much more aggressive, extreme and cruel than internet commenters who used their real names. Covering someone's face, like the guard's sunglasses, or hiding someone's name, like the prisoners and their number-names, is a very powerful way to dissociate people into new, often very scary, identities.

For leadership, Zimbardo's vague rules and non-existent oversight put the guards in an unpredictable and dangerous situation. They were untrained, they had no rules telling them how to control the prisoners, they had no boss to tell them when they were making mistakes. When people feel unsafe and unaccountable, they use brutality much more often.

In the real world, we see similar patterns. The Abu Ghraib Prison, for example, had a series of vague, weak leaders. This created stress and confusion

34 The article is available here: http://www.newyorker.com/tech/elements/the-psychology-of-online-commentshttp://www.newyorker.com/tech/elements/the-psychology-of-online-comments

among the prison guards.[35] Combined with the unpredictable and dangerous situation in Iraq, the Abu Ghraib guards began behaving very similarly to the fake guards in the Stanford Prison Experiment. Similarly, many abusive and hellish mental hospitals fail because of weak, vague leadership. [36]

The new location, the fake prison, was real enough that the students felt like real prisoners and real guards. The new place caused them to get rid of their old identities and make new identities to suit the new environment. This realness is probably why none of the boys quit or challenged Zimbardo.

You are almost certainly a good example of how location affects behavior. Do you talk to your boyfriend or girlfriend in a bar the same way you talk to your grandparents at their homes? Is your behavior on a soccer field similar to your behavior in church? Are you more or less likely to be aggressive in a video game or in your front room? Context has a very strong effect on behavior and one of the biggest jobs a teacher, manager or leader has is controlling context.

35 Leadership failures in Abu Ghraib Prison http://www.washingtonpost.com/wp-dyn/articles/A33789-2004Aug25.html

36 The most dangerous hospital in the world. http://www.bbc.com/news/magazine-30293880

Questions

Comprehension

- Explain essentialism.
- Explain what the Stanford Prison Experiment was designed to do.
- Explain why clothes, environment and leadership are important.

Exploration

- Can you explain the Stanford Prison Experiment results if you believe people are naturally good or bad?
- You are at your university wearing normal clothes. If your professor came to class, told you to climb a mountain and shoot an unknown young man in hiking clothes, would you obey?
- You are doing military service and wearing a military uniform. If your commanding officer told you to climb a mountain and shoot an unknown young man in a North Korean military uniform, would you obey?
- Is Oem Hong-gil naturally brave?
- How should teachers deal with good students?
- How should managers deal with bad workers?

Project

- The Stanford Prison Experiment is an example of people getting worse because of a bad environment. Find and explain an example of someone getting better because of a new environment.

When Others Dehumanize You 18

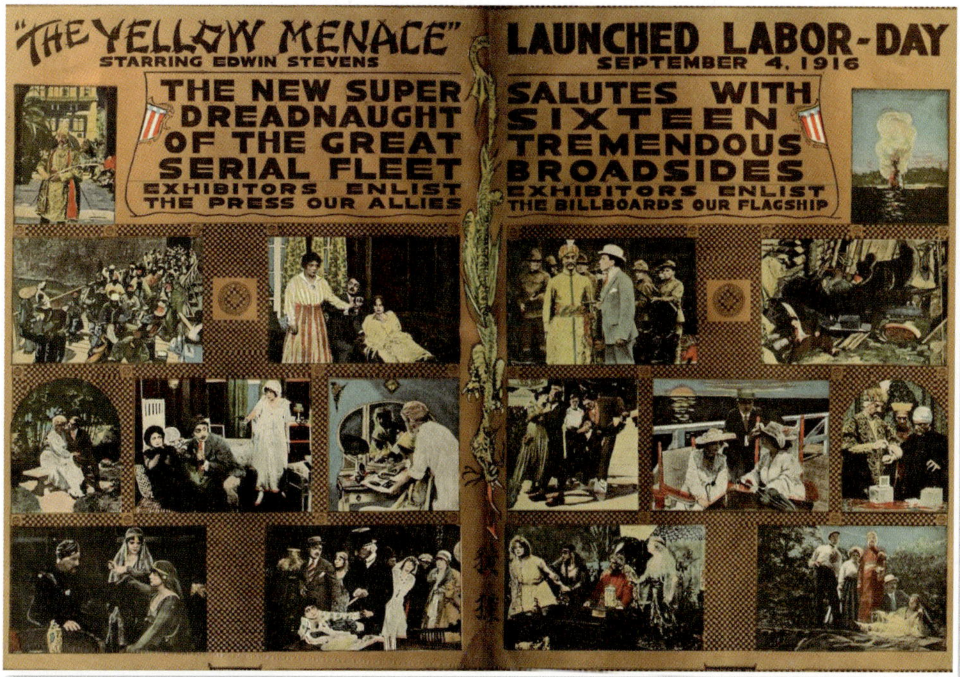

Main Questions	Should you treat people as individuals or representatives of groups?
	How do you feel when other people use essentialism on you?
	How important are categories of human beings?
	How often do you use essentialism?
	How did poor Americans view Asian people in the late 19th century?

Vocabulary	Labor Unions	Superstition	Inevitable
	Minority	Swarm	Insidious
	Heathen	Prosecution	

The Yellow Scare

From the middle of the 19th century until the early 20th century, millions of East Asian people moved to the United States. Most lived in California, Oregon and Washington and, in those states, they were very unpopular.

Labor unions believed that Asians, people like you, were job-stealing criminals. Poor whites saw the East Asian immigrants, people like you, as rapists, drug addicts and murderers. Black, Hispanic and Irish Americans thought East Asians, people like you, were weird, **superstitious** and violent. Most poor Americans agreed that East Asians--your ancestors--were essentially evil and dangerous. The rich businessmen thought differently, they believed that East Asians were naturally good as cheap labor.

The labor unions, poor whites and **minorities** joined together to get rid of "the Mongolian Races" - Chinese, Japanese, Koreans and Mongolians. First they made it illegal for the Mongolian Races to work in mines. Later, they created laws making it illegal for members of the Mongolian Races to have jobs in any large companies or with the government. In 1882, labor unions, poor whites and minorities succeeded in passing the "Chinese Exclusion Act," a law that made it illegal for any Chinese people to immigrate to the US.

Labor union leader and anti-Asian activist Samuel Gompers

However, members of the "Mongolian Races" didn't just leave the United States. Many had families, many couldn't afford to return to Asia. As such, Americans continued to find ways to protect themselves from the "threat" of Asians. This time was called the Yellow Scare.

The following article is from 1900. In it, labor union leader Samuel Gompers and co-author Herman Gutstadt argue that Americans should get rid of all "Mongolians." Remember, Gompers and Gutstadt are talking about you.

Meat vs. Rice

American Manhood Against Asiatic Coolieism. Which Shall Survive?

While we have previously tried to ban only the Chinese, we now know that all the Mongolian races, Chinese, Japanese, Koreans and Hindus, are a menaces. They all attempt to import their **insidious** customs into our Republic. Because we failed to ban all the Asiatic races, Japanese, Koreans and Hindus have mistakenly come to believe that they are welcome in our nation.

They have come in **swarms**, like poisonous bees. 30,226 Asiatics arrived in the last year alone. Give the Mongolian races two or three decades and the Asian menace will outnumber white Christians.

The Asian problem began when mining companies in California needed cheap workers. At this time, there weren't enough white people to work in the mines. The Mongolian races didn't make huge problems at that time. However, you shouldn't think they helped California grow. White people would have been much better. A famous California doctor explained the Asiatic "help" this way.

"California 'growing' with the Asian population is like a child growing with a tumor. When the child becomes an adult, that 'growth' will kill him."

The Asiatic races in America, because they are so close with crime, depend on "Tongs."[37] Tongs are virtual slave organizations. Together with greedy companies, who don't hate the Mongolian Races, they ignore morality and treat the immigrants like cattle. Like all Asiatic organizations, there is rampant crime with the Tongs. Even the Mongolian **heathens** would be happier if we made them leave because then the Tongs couldn't hurt them.

37 A Tong is a kind of Mafia. They helped smuggle immigrants into and out of California.

The Tongs use murder and intimidation to control the Asiatics. However, we think we should acquit the Tongs of their crimes. This is because murder and slavery are normal parts of the Asiatic mind and culture. The correct choice is expulsion, not **prosecution**. That said, the next time you hear some confused white person compliment the "friendly little yellow people," remember all the violence.

They are also invaders. They started in the mines, but now the Asiatic menace has spread into all the industries, stealing jobs from white Christians. Every Asiatic with a job means that there's another white woman who can't work. Every heathen, criminal Asiatic store destroys a moral, white store. Anywhere the Asians go they destroy the white laborer's entire life.

In order to steal the jobs, Asiatic heathens will work so cheaply that white people can't compete. Then, when all the white workers are destroyed, the Mongolian Races will demand extremely high pay and destroy the white companies as well. It's only a matter of time before the Asiatic heathens completely take over the economy.

The Asians are cunning but inferior to the white man in arts, philosophy and science. They are hard workers, but in the same way that slaves work hard. They are gifted in commerce, but, just like mold or bacteria, they always spread. Many islands in South Asia have already been completely overrun with Chinese, Japanese and Koreans.

The Asian hordes are spreading over the world. The white, Christian civilization will meet it. When these great waves of white and yellow collide, who will survive? We cannot know. Already, the heathens have overrun our beautiful state, Hawaii. San Francisco is their next target.

- Gompers and Godstadt

Analysis

How do you feel after reading this article? Are you feeling angry and insulted? Imagine how people would react if Barack Obama gave a speech like this. Imagine what would happen if Vladimir Putin said these things.

So why?

I’d like you to think about why I included this article in the book. It isn’t very well written. It has several logical problems. The argument is contradictory and, if you really think about it, kind of stupid.

Essentialism needs two things to work. Essentialism must assume people don’t really change and it must assume that *types of people* are more important than *individual people*. Gompers and Gutstadt took those essentialist assumptions and used them on you.

Notice how Gompers and Gutstadt never talk about an individual member of “the Mongolian Races.” They never talk about Ling the Chinese farmer, Toshi the Japanese store owner or Gwang-jin the Korean miner because, to an essentialist, *they’re all the same.* Gompers and Gutstadt never discuss the possibility that Asian immigrants might become American citizens, Christians or unionized workers. After all, the essentialist believes that people never really change.

This kind of essentialist mindset is dehumanizing. It makes growth and development impossible. It takes huge groups of people and makes them into a label. When you treat your future students or workers as **inevitably** good, inevitably bad or inevitably smart, you are doing something very similar to what Gompers and Gutstadt just did to you.

Questions

Comprehension:

- What was the Yellow Scare?
- What were Gompers and Godstadt trying to do?
- Who are the "Mongolian Races?"

Exploration:

- Write about the feelings you experienced reading Gompers and Godstadt's article.
- Are Gompers and Godstadt being unfair? If so, how?
- Was the Yellow Scare rational? Did the horrible results Gompers and Godstadt predicted happen?
- Why don't Gompers and Godstadt ever talk about individual Asian people?
- Can you think of any modern people like Gompers and Godstadt?
- Is it possible to have essentialist beliefs that are better than Gompers and Godstadt's essential beliefs?

Project:

- Write a letter to Gompers and Godstadt.

____

____

____

____

____

____

____

Dehumanizing Others

Main Questions	What kinds of essentialism are most common in your life?
	Is it easier to find essentialism in other people than in yourself?
	What people do you think are most vulnerable to essentialism in Korea?
	How can you respect your followers' humanity?

Vocabulary	Dehumanize	Self Esteem	Substance Abuse
	Stereotype	Heritage	Labeling

Gompers and Gutsdadt Aren't the Only Essentialists

It doesn't feel very good when people like Gompers and Gutstadt treat you like like animals. It sucks when they ignore your individual characteristics and use their essentialism to generalize. People like Gompers and Gutstadt should fill you with anger. Please remember that feeling as you read this chapter.

Essentialism in Your Future

You need to remember this feeling because Gompers and Gutstadt aren't the only ones who use essentialism to **dehumanize** other people. Indeed, as future leaders, you will have to manage essentialism in your students, your bosses and your coworkers. Essentialism will be common in your workplace.

Most people try to be fair. Most of your bosses and coworkers will make a good attempt to treat the people around them well, however, there are some common problems you need to be aware of.

For example, according to the Anti-Defamation League, South Korea has more essentialistic views of Jews than most developed nations. 53% of Korean citizens polled had **stereotypical** attitudes about Jews, compared to 23% of Japanese and 20% of Chinese. Further, international couples - particularly Chinese, Southeast Asian or Indian - are consistently portrayed as unhappy, tragic and dangerous on TV.

The Atlanta Black Star likewise lists South Korea as one of the 8 worst countries in the world for black people. I personally know two black academy teachers who were fired "because parents don't like black people."

Stereotypes for Chinese people are "noisy, smelly and dishonest." Southeast Asians are sometimes stereotyped as "lazy, slow and stupid." 80% of immigrant laborers in Korea have been insulted for their **heritage**.[38]

Jang Wee-yeon, a Chinese celebrity in Korea, discussed his experiences with essentialism.[39] He mentioned the annoyance he felt being insulted for his race. Even North Koreans suffer from essentialist attitudes. Many can't even get

38 Essentialism in South Korea. http://m.news.naver.com/comment/list.nhn?gno=news053%2c0000020930&aid=0000020930&mode=LSD&oid=053&sid1=102&backUrl=%2fmain.nhn%3fmode%3dLSD%26sid1%3d102

39 Jang Wee-yeon http://m.entertain.naver.com/comment/list?oid=109&aid=0002884538

job interviews because essentialist company directors assume they will always fail.[40] The problems the character "Jiwon" faced in 국가대표 2 are not that uncommon.

Websites like Ilbe are even more severe. Indeed, if you become teachers, you will find that many of your students go to Ilbe to express their hatred.[41] You will find hostile and racist discussions of Japanese people, "Yankee Princesses," Southeast Asians, Indian people and North Korean defectors. You will find attitudes very similar to Gompers and Gutsdadt. Indeed, in all of these cases, the essentialists ignore the individual people and focus on **labeling**.

Why This Matters

2% of human beings are gay. You will teach, manage or work with a gay person almost every day. According to the World Health Organization, 10.3% of Korean men suffer from **substance abuse** problems.[42] This means many, many of your followers will go home to alcoholic households. 1,800,000 foreigners live in South Korea right now. The government estimates that there will be 17,000,000 foreigners in South Korea by 2060, or about the time you retire. [43] You will have to deal with Kopinos and Chinese and Japanese people.

You will manage workers from rich families and poor families. You will teach

40 North Koreans unable to get jobs. http://m.news.naver.com/read.nhn?mode=LSD&mid=sec&sid1=104&oid=040&aid=0000115079

41 Ilbe hates Little Psy http://www.koreabang.com/2013/stories/little-psy-subject-of-online-racial-hatred.html

42 Alcohol use in South Korea http://www.who.int/substance_abuse/publications/global_alcohol_report/profiles/kor.pdf

43 Immigrants in South Korea http://www.mt.co.kr/view/mtview.php?type=1&no=2015122721551652955&outlink=1

students from gangster families and students whose parents are divorced. Some of your followers will have no **self-esteem** and some will have too much self-esteem. Some will succeed early in life and then fail as they age. Some will fail when they are young and succeed later.

As a leader, your duty is to help all of these people. If you treat your Kopino students like essential representatives of the Philippines, you will not be a good teacher for them. If you treat workers from bad families like they are essentially criminals, you will harm them very badly. If you don't recognize and control the essentialism in your workplace, you will be treating your followers the way Gompers and Gutsdadt treated you last chapter.

Questions

Comprehension

- Why is Jung Wee-yeon unhappy?
- How will Korean demographics change in the future?

Exploration

- Compare your feelings now with your feelings after reading Gompers and Gutsdadt's article.
- Compare and contrast Gompers and Gutsdadt's article with this, taken from a protest in Seoul.

한국을 다인종/다민족 국가로 만들고자 이분화 정책을 반대합니다. 한국에 체류하는 외국인 노동자와 결혼 이민자들을 주요 대상으로 시행하는 현 정책에 대해 국민의 다양한 의견을 수렴해 주세요.

1. 외국인 노동자들은 눈 높은 한국인들을 대신해 3D업종을 대신 채워 묵묵히 일해주는 존재가 아닙니다. 한국인들의 3D 업종 기피현상은 임금과 노동환경 개선이 해결책이지 이국인노동자의 유입이 아닙니다. 그들은 월급 대부분을 모국으로 송금해버리기 때문에 내수경제에 도움이 되지않고 노동환경 개선과 최저임금 상승을 방해합니다. 또 외국인노동자들은 받는 임금을 송금하면 환율상 큰 돈이 되기 때문에 기꺼이 한국에서 일할뿐입니다. 똑같은 임금을 받아도 외국인 노동자에게는 큰 돈이지만 국내 노동자에게는 적은 돈일 뿐입니다. 이들을 위해 다문화를 장려하고 또 더 나아가 불법체류자 자녀교육 생활을 지원한다넌 오히려 외국인 노동자듬과 불법체류자들이 놀러갈 수 있도록 도와주는 꼴입니다. 내국인에게 씌워진 "3D 업종을 기피하고 편한 일만 찾는" 누명을 벗기고 정당한 환경에서 정당한 임금을 받을 수 있게 국가가 장려해야 합니다. 외국인 노동자들을 수용하는 방법으로만 의존하면 결곡 고용시장은 교란되고 경제가 흔들린 뿐입니다. <u>자국민을 먼저 생각하고 보호해 주세요.</u>

2. 현재 한국에 체류하는 결혼 이민자 중 약 89% 여성이고 그 중 결혼중개 업체를 통해 들어오는 경우가 많습니다. 하지만 짧은 만남 일정과 중개과정 등, 특성상 한계를 가져 국적취득을 목적으로한 결혼, 가출, 가정폭력, 문화습득의 어려움 등 많은 위협과 문제점 (높은 이혼율)들은 낳고 있습니다. 상대방 국가들 조차 인신매매적 성격이 다소 짙다고 보는 국제 중개 업체를 통한 실시하는 것을 바람직하지만 경제적, 경제적 지원을 해주는 것은 오히려 내국인 가정에 대한 역차별입니다. "자연스러운" 국제 결혼보다 인위적인 중개업체를 통한 국제결혼을 장려하면 자녀를 "한국인"으로 키울 의무가 있으며 이들에게 (가정에 문화가 공존하던 안 하던) 다문화 가정이라는 이름으로 구별하거나 특혜를 주면 그에 대한 이질감과 내국인의 반감만 커질 수 밖에 없습니다.

"우리 나라는 단일민족은 아닐지언정 하나의 공통된 문화를 지키고 살아온 나라입니다. 이민자 국가가 아닌 한국에 다문화사회를 계획하신다면 좀 더 신중하게 생각해주세요."

20 How Leaders Should Treat Followers

Main Questions	
	How should you treat students, workers or co-workers?
	Should you treat different kinds of people differently?
	What makes human beings unique?
	What will education be like in the future?
	How can we avoid essentialism?

Vocabulary			
	Learned Helplessness	Ziggurat	Instinct
	Illiterate	Naturally Inclined	Psychological Fragility

What it Means to Be Human

If someone says "cows are stupid" they are probably not going to offend the cows. "Dogs smell bad" is almost always a true statement. It is very easy to predict the life and behavior of a corn plant based on the essential qualities of a corn plant.

Dogs will run and chase mice but they will not build a **ziggurat**. Cows will eat grass and move in groups but they will not compose a symphony. Corn will grow wherever you plant it but will never read a book. Plants and animals do not choose very much. Instead they use **instinct** and their genetic programming. There's really no problem with being a corn essentialist, cow essentialist or dog essentialist.

People are different. Whether you explain our special status with your religious beliefs, scientific beliefs, traditions or philosophical beliefs, the conclusion is the same. Human beings can do too many things, they are too complicated and too mysterious to accurately predict. Human beings are the animals that choose.

People can choose to run and chase mice but they can also choose to build bridges. A baby born into a farming family can become a president, a race car driver or a gangster. Genghis Khan, probably the most important person of the last 1000 years, began as a minor leader from an **illiterate** tribe. Josef Stalin was a failed priest who chose to join the Communist Party. Marie Curie was born into a family of outlaw Polish school teachers before choosing to become a great scientist in France.

This complexity, this ability to choose, is a fundamental part of being human. We don't know what people will do or what they will become in the future. When we use essentialism, we are basically treating people like dogs, cows or corn.

Attitudes and Techniques

Avoiding essentialism is difficult. Most people are **naturally inclined** to thinking essentialistically. It's so easy to do. However, it is possible to go beyond essentialism with practice and a few techniques. You must remember, basically, that choice is what makes us human.

Focus on Things People Can Control

While teaching at a kindergarten, I watched the other teachers praise a little girl (we'll call her Nina) almost every day. They would lead Nina to the office and hold her, telling her that she was pretty. The teachers gave her extra attention. When Nina didn't do her homework or did poorly on a test, the teachers excused her. She was pretty, after all.

In my opinion and according to a lot of research, those teachers were really, really damaging Nina's chance at success. Prettiness, after all, isn't something Nina can control. Maybe she will always be pretty, but probably not. However, being pretty is the most important thing her teachers and parents focused on. How terrible will her life be if she grows up ugly, or even average-looking?

Even worse, by teaching Nina that prettiness is the most important thing, those teachers were teaching her that choices aren't important. When Nina has challenges later in life, she will believe that her essential prettiness is the only way to solve those problems. Indeed, even in kindergarten, Nina was falling behind other students and feeling helpless.

A similar thing happened at one of my old jobs. The owner would yell at her workers and punish them frequently. When the workers would ask what to do, she would give vague and useless answers like "you need to be smarter," "just make it work" or "if you were a better person you would know."

Her workers felt hopeless and discouraged since there was no way to "be smarter" or "be a better person" that they could find. The woman who worked next to me quit her job after only 4 months, my supervisor also quit in only six months. I also quit in less than a year. Not surprisingly, my supervisor drove her business into the ground.

Indeed, there's a term for this process - **learned helplessness.** Learned helplessness is when a person or animal learns that they can never fix problems. For example, if we punish a dog without reason and prevent the dog from escaping, it will eventually learn that it has no power - that it is helpless. After enough training, an animal that has learned helplessness will accept punishment even if you give it the opportunity to escape. Nina and my coworkers were learning that success and failure, pain and pleasure, were outside their control.

Learned Helplessness

Stage One - Inescapable Punishment > Subject Learns They Have No Control > Subject Lies Down Passively, Accepts Punishment
Stage Two - **Escapable** Punishment > Subject Lies Down Passively, Accepts Punishment

What if the teachers had ignored Nina's cuteness? What if my boss had given her employees specific things to change? What if the teachers had judged Nina on her actions? What if the boss had made clear rules for reward and punishment?

Nina can control how hard she works. She can change how she plays with other children. She can learn to study more efficiently and she has the opportunity to get better at art. How much more power would Nina have if the teachers had focused on the things she can control?

Employees can do paperwork differently. They can come to work early or drink less. They can learn sales techniques or get better at dealing with angry customers. How much more effective would the employees have been if my old boss had focused on the things they could control?

We have spoken about "bad" essentialism like the Yellow Scare and Ilbe, but praising people for essential qualities is actually just as bad. Let's look at some reasons why that is.

According to New York Magazine[44], praising children for being smart, pretty or talented is an excellent way to make those children **psychologically fragile**, nervous and afraid of risk. In other words, essentialist praise is a great way to make cowards. On the other hand, if we praise children for effort, those children tend to grow stronger, more confident and braver. Adults are exactly the same. Praising a worker for things he or she can control correlates with greater productivity, happiness and engagement.

After all, if we are essentially *good/bad/smart/whatever*, what's the point of trying something different? However, if we teach people that they have the ability to change, those people will go home believing they have the power to adapt, to grow, to overcome challenges. If you can change, why not try something different?

As such, leaders should focus almost exclusively on things that workers and students can control. Being specific helps with this. Students should be evaluated on effort while teachers carefully ignore their IQ scores. Workers should be praised or criticized on accomplishments, not rated on talent. There's no point in criticizing an athlete for being too short, but there is a point in developing technique.

Examples of Useful Praise:

1. You worked hard on (specific thing).
2. I'm impressed that you came up with your own (specific) idea.
3. That was a brave (specific) decision.
4. I'm proud of you for trying some (specific) new thing.

44 The dangers of praising children for essential characteristics. http://nymag.com/news/features/27840/

Examples of Useful Criticism:

1. I don't think you tried hard enough on (specific thing).
2. You just copied somebody else' s (specific thing). Don't be lazy.
3. You need to push yourself to do (specific thing).
4. I think you can do better if you (specific action).

Examples of Damaging Praise:

1. You are so smart.
2. Your talent makes you special.
3. You're so pretty.
4. You are just so good.

Examples of Damaging Criticism:

1. You just aren't smart enough.
2. You don't have a talent for this.
3. I think you will fail a lot.
4. You're just a bad person.

Questions

Comprehension

- What is learned helplessness?
- How are learned helplessness and essentialism connected?
- Why is choice important?

Exploration

- What are some specific ways you can encourage your followers to make choices?
- How much of the praise and criticism that you get is useful?
- Who, in your life, has given you the most power?
- You are leading a group of poor people from bad families. How will you design your lessons or plans differently?

Group Activity

- Fill in the following sentences with a partner.

  a) Chinese people are ______________________________________
  b) Men are ______________________________________
  c) Rich people are ______________________________________

- Were your answers fair to rich people, men and the Chinese?

____
____
____
____
____
____

Dr. McN, Professor CL and Using Power

21

German chancellor Angela Merkel is a master of using power constructively.

Main Questions	Are good people always good leaders?
	Should all people use the same morality?
	What specific things make good leaders?
	How do bad leaders fail?

Vocabulary	Receding Hairline	Appalling
	Vulgar	Controversial
	Servile	Anthropology

I'd like to tell you about the best and worst teachers I ever had. This is partly because I feel the story is interesting, partly because I want to recognize and thank the previously mentioned best teacher, but the biggest reason I'm telling this story is because I believe it illustrates how to both succeed and fail at leadership.

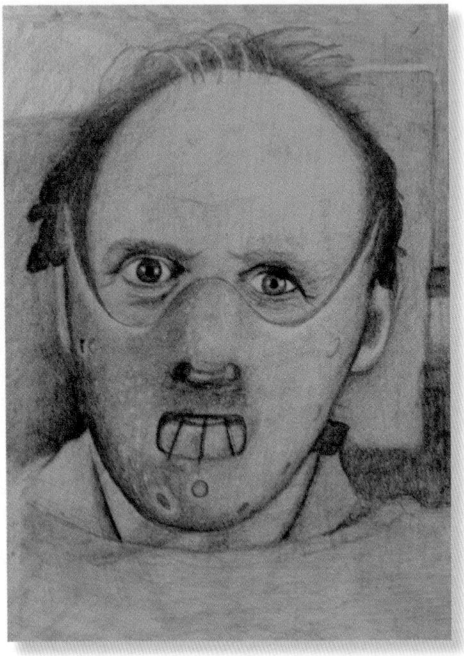

This is more or less what Dr. McN looked like to me when I first met him.

Dr. McN taught honors English 1 and AP English 4, both subjects I disliked, at my high school. He looked a lot like Hannibal Lecter, which is exactly what we called him behind his back. He had a severely **receding hairline** which he managed to make even more severe by slicking the remaining hairs straight back. He had yellow teeth, which he liked to suck at. He hunched over like a movie monster.

His manner of speaking wasn't much better. On the first day I met him, he called me and the rest of my class "the cream of the crap." (Cream of the crop means "best of the group." Cream of the crap - use your imagination.) Within the first week, Dr. McN had called my education **appalling**, my taste in books **vulgar** and my thinking lazy. It was not until my senior year I got a compliment out of him and that compliment went something like this:

"You're a good student, when and if you pull your head out of your *butt.*[45]"

I am still a combative, cocky and reckless person. In high school, I was really combative, really cocky and stupidly reckless - much worse in every way. I wanted to fight everybody, all the time. I thought I was the smartest person alive and I did something stupidly, pointlessly brave about once a week. I feared pretty much nothing - except Dr. McN.

45 Dr. McN didn't actually say "butt," but something more vulgar.

Professor CL, on the other hand, made a point to welcome me to her class. She taught a **controversial** subject in social science and, as such, told me that she didn't want me to feel personally attacked by the things she would show us. Professor CL smiled when she greeted students to the class. She put her hand on students' shoulders. When the subject matter became controversial, she would say things like "I don't mean to offend ~, but this is our belief."

This is how Professor CL looked to me when I first met her.

Professor CL had words of encouragement for all the students, all the time. She dressed in mild, neutral colors, played soothing music and had a soft voice.

I was genuinely interested in her subject and the controversial things she said didn't offend me in the least. At the time, I was strongly considering a career in social science, so I had prepared for the class beforehand, without being asked. Professor CL, as opposed to Dr. McN, didn't intimidate me at all.

It might surprise you to learn that Dr. McN was the best teacher I ever had the privilege of meeting. I have never worked harder for a teacher than I worked for Dr. McN. He convinced me to abandon my simplistic moral beliefs. He, more than anyone else, taught me to think critically. When I was lazy or thoughtless, Dr. McN told me. Dr. McN, almost alone, got me interested in philosophy, literature and art. He demanded that I challenge him and attacked me when my challenges weren't well prepared. His preparation was excellent. When I did manage to surprise him with questions, he would find information and analysis before the next class. His rules were clear and consistent. His goal was always the same - to improve his students as much as possible. He took me, a cocky, reckless kid and made something more - I am eternally in his debt.

By contrast, Professor CL wasted three incredibly frustrating months of my life. She angered me with a false **servility**. Professor CL would always talk about how she was open to ideas and challenges then, when I presented those ideas and challenges, she would get angry and mark down my grade. She lost my respect with poor preparation. Countless times, Professor CL would tell us to agree with her opinion and present either no evidence or stupid evidence. She said she wanted to teach us about equality, but in practice, her entire focus was on calling certain groups evil. She was afraid of outside sources. She forbid us to discuss biology and **anthropology** because those things conflicted with her beliefs. She used her power as professor to silence opponents and, in doing so, showed herself weak. Her rules were hidden and changeable, just like her goals.

At the end of the semester, I helped to get Professor CL fired. I'm still proud of that.

Friedrich Nietzsche, Jean-Paul Sartre and Hannah Arendt believed the morality of leaders and followers should be different.

One of the most commonly held assumptions in the 21st century is that we are all answerable to the same, universal standard of morality. Being kind, being humble, being agreeable, being merciful, being charitable these are the marks of goodness in both teachers and prison guards, small children and retired business people, presidents and janitors.

I want you to question this assumption.

Leadership is largely power. A good teacher or official inspires his or her follower. An average leader uses coercion. A bad teacher or official neither inspires nor coerces, but allows rebellion. Followers will see the good leader as richly deserving power, the average leader as sufficient and a bad leader as stupid, weak and contemptible. It is then our duty, as leaders and future leaders, to understand the ways power works, how to use power and how power differs from our ideas of good and bad.

In each chapter, we will examine a different story of leadership. Most of these examples will not come from education or business. Indeed, the first three chapters will focus on a Chinese general, an Italian politician and two American sociologists. We then will discuss how you, future teachers and officials, can use these concepts in your own workplaces.

Questions:

Exploration:

- Think of the teachers who taught you the most and the teachers who taught you the least. What, specifically, did they do differently?
- Professor CL appears to have many moral good points. Dr. McN appears to have many fewer. How can you explain this?
- What are the most important qualities for leaders to have?

Activity:

- Fill in the following chart. Is there any relationship between goodness and leadership ability?

	Good Person	Bad Person	Good Leader	Bad Leader
Park Jung-hee				
Genghis Khan				
Steve Jobs				
Queen Elizabeth I				
Jimmy Carter				
King Seon-jo				
Erwin Rommel				
Wu Zetian				
Theodore Roosevelt				
Che Guevara				
Maximillien Robespierre				

Sun Tzu and the Concubine Army

22

Main Questions	How can you get power over other people?
	What are important techniques for keeping your power?
	What should you use your power for?
	Is it better for a leader to follow his own rules or to lead arbitrarily?
	Is the consent of the followers useful?

Vocabulary	Tyranny	Concubine
	Legitimacy	Execution
	Commitment	

Power is a kind of scary topic. When most people think about power, they imagine crazed dictators or evil bosses who use terror and tyranny to control their victims. While **tyranny** is a possible way to use power, it's not a very stable or intelligent way to use your strength.
This next article is about how to look at and use power systematically. Sun-tzu, the famous Chinese general and theorist, approaches the problem of building a military with the intent to build a clear and consistent structure of responsibility. As you read, it might be useful to think of Sun-tzu as less a general and more of a social engineer.

This story seems very simple, but I promise it is not. Nothing Sun-tzu does in this story is an accident and most of his actions are doing two or three things at the same time. Pay special attention to the italicized analysis.

Sun-tzu and the Concubine Army
By Grand Historian Ssu-ma Ch'ien

Sun Tzu was a native of the Ch'i State. His "Art of War" made him famous and earned the attention of Ho Lu, King of Wu.

Ho Lu said to him "I have carefully read your 13 chapters. May I test your theory of managing soldiers?

Sun Tzu replied "you may."

Ho Lu asked "Can I use women for the test?"

Sun Tzu again said "you may."

Arrangements were made to bring 180 ladies out of the palace. Sun Tzu divided them into two groups and placed one of the King's favorite **concubines** in charge of each.

By dividing the women into groups and appointing leaders, Sun-tzu is creating a system of responsibility. Leaders must create clear roles for their followers if they hope to succeed.

He then asked the ladies to take spears in their hands and spoke thus:

"I assume you know the difference between front and back, right hand and left hand?"

The women said "yes."

Sun Tzu went on. "When I say 'eyes front,' you must look straight ahead. When I say 'turn left,' you must face towards your left hand. When I say 'right turn,' you must face towards your right hand. When I say 'about turn,' you must face towards your back." Again the women agreed.

These instructions are very simple, but Sun Tzu is making sure the women understand the rules. So first, he builds a system of responsibility and now he is filling that system with clear and consistent rules. He also gets the women to agree freely. This is important because getting followers to agree to your leadership is an excellent way to build ***legitimacy.***

Having thus explained the commands, Sun Tzu began the drill. To the sound of drums he gave the order "right turn." But the women only laughed. Sun Tzu said "if words of command are not clear and distinct, if the orders are not thoroughly understood, then the general is at fault."

This seems odd if you really think about it. Sun Tzu's instructions were very simple and he explained them carefully beforehand. However, by taking the blame himself, he is showing the women two things. First, he is responsible and controlled by rules just like they are. Second, he is reasonable. The concubines will not be punished for honest mistakes or misunderstandings.

So he started the drilling again, this time giving the order "left turn," whereupon the women once more burst into fits of laughter. Sun Tzu said "if words of command are not clear and distinct, if orders are not thoroughly understood, the general is to blame. But if his orders are clear and the soldiers nonetheless disobey, then it is the fault of the officers."

So saying, he ordered the leaders of the two groups to be executed. Now, the King of Wu was watching and he saw that his favorite concubines were about to be executed, he was greatly alarmed and hurried to send this message.

"I am satisfied that General Sun Tzu can handle troops. If I am bereft of these two concubines, my food and drink will lose their flavor. I wish you do not execute my concubines."

Sun Tzu answered "His Majesty has entrusted me as a general of his troops. It is my duty to prepare the troops as best I can. To fulfill my duty, there are certain of His Majesty's commands I am unable to accept."

Sun Tzu has accomplished two more things here. First, he showed the concubines that there are consequences to disobeying the rules. Second, he showed that the rules and system of responsibility are more important than everyone, including the king.

Accordingly, Sun Tzu had the two concubines executed and chose two more concubines to lead the groups of women. When this had been done, he again sounded the drums and began the drills. This time the women performed all of the general's commands perfectly, turning right or left, marching ahead or marching back, kneeling or standing with perfect accuracy and precision. Then Sun Tzu sent a messenger to the King.

"Your soldiers, Sire, are now properly drilled and disciplined. They are ready for Your Majesty's inspection. They can be put to any use their king may desire. Order them to go through fire and water, they will not disobey."

But the King replied "let our general cease drilling and return to the camp. I have no desire to come down and inspect the soldiers."

Sun Tzu replied to the King of Wu, saying "the King loves only words and cannot make his words into deeds."

Sun Tzu criticizes the king here because the king showed a lack of commitment. Effective leaders, like Sun Tzu, must show their followers that they are committed to leadership. The king's lack of commitment is thus a threat to the entire project.

After that, King Ho Lu of Wu saw that Sun Tzu was one who knew how to handle an army and appointed him general.

Questions:

Exploration:

- Does Sun Tzu appear cruel to you? If he seems cruel, explain a better way to train the concubines. If he doesn't appear cruel to you, explain why he was justified in killing the women.
- Why does Sun Tzu ask the concubines twice? Why doesn't he execute the concubine leaders after the first failure?
- Why does Sun Tzu refuse the king's request to save the concubines?
- Aside from fear, why do the concubines follow Sun Tzu?

Group Activity

- What techniques from Sun Tzu can you use to lead? Share your answers with a partner.

23 Whether it is Better to be Loved or Feared

Japanese commander Hatazo Adachi surrenders to Australian admiral Horace Robertson in 1945.

Main Questions	Is it good enough to be nice when you are a leader?
	Can you be an effective leader if you focus on being tough?
	Is it better to be loved or feared?
	Why is hatred dangerous for leaders?

Vocabulary	Ad hoc	Clement
	Anarchy	Fickle
	Covetous	Justification
	Boundless	

In my experience, new college graduates have very little idea how to get or use power. Many of my education students seem to believe that if they are kind enough, students will follow them. I've had several business and economics students who believed that being tough would suffice.

When these graduates go out into the real world, their ideas of niceness and toughness don't work. Usually, the graduates feel lost and confused. Usually, they try to make strategies **ad hoc** to deal with the new realities of their workplaces. I hope, as you read this article from 16th century Italian politician Niccolo Machiavelli, you can begin to understand how power works independently of being tough or nice. If so, your transition into the workplace could become a lot easier.

Excerpt from The Prince
by Niccolo Machiavelli

I say that every prince ought to desire to be considered **clement** and not cruel. Nevertheless he ought to take care not to misuse this clemency. Cesare Borgia was considered cruel but his cruelty reconciled the Romagna, unified it, and restored it to peace and loyalty. If you think of this correctly, you will see that he was much more merciful than the Florentine people who, not wanting to seem cruel, allowed Pistoia to be destroyed.[46]

Therefore a prince, so long as he keeps his subjects united and loyal, should not worry when others call him cruel because with a few examples of cruelty, he will be more merciful than those who, through too much mercy, allow **anarchy** to arise. This is because murders and robberies, which injure all the people, come from anarchy. In contrast, the prince's cruelty injures individuals only.

Is this good advice for a teacher? Should a teacher worry about being cruel if they have an orderly class? Should a business leader make "examples" of one or two rebellious followers so the rest can work well?

Nevertheless he ought to be slow to believe and to act, he should never show fear, but proceed in the spirit of moderation, so that too much confidence may not make him reckless and too much suspicion make him intolerable.

46 Romagna and Pistoia are both Italian cities. Cesare Borgia was famous for being cruel but effective. The Florentines were famous for being kind but ineffective. More information about Cesare Borgia. http://terms.naver.com/entry.nhn?docId=1102436&cid=40942&categoryId=34317

Upon this a question arises: whether it be better to be loved than feared or feared than loved? I would answer that it is best to be feared and loved, but, because it is difficult to have both things at the same time, is much safer to be feared if you cannot have both. This is because men are ungrateful, **fickle**, false, cowardly and **covetous**. When you succeed, they will swear to be loyal to you but as soon as danger comes, they run away and leave you alone.

A prince who believes his people's promises and has not prepared other defenses will be ruined. This is because friendships that are obtained by payments, and not by greatness or nobility of mind, may indeed be earned, but they are not safe. When times are difficult these friendships cannot be relied upon. Men have more willingness to offend one who is beloved than one who is feared. This is because love is under the control of the follower while fear is under the control of the leaders. Therefore love is easily broken but fear never fails.

Is this true? Do allies made from generous behavior remain loyal? How about allies made from respect? How about allies made from fear? How about allies made from force?

Nevertheless a prince ought to inspire fear in such a way that, if he does not win love, he avoids hatred. A prince can survive very well being feared if he is not hated. He will not be hated so long as he doesn't steal the property or women from his people. When it is necessary for him to destroy an individual, he must do it on proper **justification** and for manifest cause.

Did Sun Tzu have proper justification and manifest cause for killing the concubine leaders?

But when a prince is with his army, then it is quite necessary for him to use cruelty, for without it he would never hold his army united or disposed to its duties.

Among the wonderful deeds of Hannibal this one is enumerated: that having led an enormous army, composed of many various races of men, to fight in foreign lands, his soldiers never revolted or disobeyed his orders. They obeyed both when Hannibal enjoyed success and when he failed.[47]

47 For more information about Hannibal Barcas visit here: http://terms.naver.com/entry.nhn?docId=1161195&cid=40942&categoryId=33471

Carthaginian leader Hannibal Barcas and Roman general Scipio Africanus fought each other in the Second Punic War. Both were excellent commanders on the level of Lee Sun-shin.

This loyalty arose from nothing else than his inhuman cruelty, which, combined with his **boundless** courage, made him both admirable and terrifying in the sight of his soldiers. Hannibal was brave, daring, inventive and brilliant, but without that cruelty, his other virtues were not sufficient to ensure loyalty. Shortsighted writers admire his deeds and then condemn the cruelty that made his amazing deeds possible.

I can prove that Hannibal's other virtues would not have been sufficient by comparing him with Scipio, that most excellent man. Scipio was Hannibal's equal in bravery, in genius and in daring but nevertheless, Scipio's army rebelled in Spain. This arose from nothing but his too great mercy. Wishing to be kind, Scipio gave his soldiers more licence than is consistent with military discipline.[48] For this he was criticized in the Senate and called the corrupter of the Roman soldiery.

When the Locrians (a minor Greek tribe under Rome's protection) were laid

48 For more information about Scipio Africanus visit here: http://terms.naver.com/entry.nhn?docId=1719395&cid=43077&categoryId=43077

waste by a legate of Scipio, Scipio did not have the legate punished, owing entirely to his easy nature. (Scipio's officer attacked the Locrians but Scipio, wanting to be kind, did not punish the officer. Legate = officer.)

The Senate, wishing to excuse Scipio's mistakes, said there were many men who knew much better how to behave than to fix the bad behavior of others. This mercy, if the Senate had not forced Scipio to change, would have destroyed the fame and glory of Scipio.

You will probably not lead armies, but do you think Machiavelli's advice for armies would be helpful during a crisis in your company, department or school?

Returning to the question of being feared or loved, I come to the conclusion that, because men love according to their own will and fear according to the prince's, a wise prince should establish himself on things he can control. He must endeavour only to avoid hatred, as is noted.

Questions:

Activity:

- I made the following lists of ways to be kind and cruel. Please add at least one more way to be cruel and hated, cruel but not hated, kind and hated, kind but not hated.

  a) Types of cruelty that inspire hatred: Capriciousness, humiliation, inferiority complexes
  b) Types of cruelty that do not inspire hatred: Ruthlessness, severity, high standards
  c) Types of kindness that inspire hatred: Favoritism, giving unearned gifts, fake friendship
  d) Types of kindness that do not inspire hatred: Thorough but conditional forgiveness, giving earned gifts (particularly the gift of trust), recognizing achievement

Exploration:

- Do you agree with Machiavelli that a leader (teacher) can control fear but can't control love?
- Is it better to be cruel like Hannibal or kind like Scipio?
- After reading this section and Sun Tzu's section, analyze why Dr. McN was a good teacher and Professor CL was not.

24 French and Raven's Five Forms of Power

Main Questions	What are the sources of power in a workplace?
	How can people as different as Psy and Ban Gi-moon have so much power?
	How much punishment should you use?
	How should you use rewards?

Vocabulary	Coercive	Referent
	Mandate	Hierarchy
	Satiation	Conman
	Devolve	Have a Stake

Almost everyone has some power. Even very ordinary people have power over children, younger siblings, the mentally challenged and the very old. You, as future leaders, will have considerably more power than this. If you become a teacher, you will lead hundreds or thousands of young people every year. If you become a public official, your decisions will impact entire neighborhoods.

If you understand how this power works and where it comes from, you have a much better chance of being Sun Tzu. If you don't understand, you could end up like Professor CL. As such, let's look into the sources of your power in the office.

Understanding Power

John French and Bertram Raven, in 1959, published one of the most famous studies of power. In it, they identified five basic sources of power:

1. **Legitimate** - This power comes from a person's position and title.
2. **Reward** - This results from one person's ability to give gifts, rewards or even bribes.
3. **Expert** - This is based on a person's superior skill and knowledge.
4. **Referent** - This is the result of a person's charisma, attractiveness or fame.
5. **Coercive** - This comes from the ability to punish.

You can further divide these types of power into two categories, positional power and personal power. Positional power includes legitimate power, **coercive** power and reward power. Personal power includes expert and **referent** powers.

Positional Power Sources

Legitimate Power

A president, prime minister, or monarch has legitimate power. So does a CEO, a teacher or a fire chief. Electoral **mandates**, social **hierarchies,** cultural norms, and organizational structure all provide the basis for legitimate power. Legitimate power is always a function of your place in the social system.

This type of power is often unstable. If you lose your job or your title, your power quickly vanishes as well. Further, legitimate power has clear limits. If you, for example, derive your power from your position as a security expert, people will probably listen to you when you talk about safety and crime. However, if you try to influence them about making investments or educating children, most people will ignore you.

Many leaders in Korea love legitimate power. In your experience, are they good leaders?

Further, this kind of power is not based on your personal abilities or accomplishments. When people listen to a policeman, for example, they aren't actually listening to the person, they are listening to the person's uniform. The policeman can be corrupt, stupid or inexperienced, but people still listen because of his uniform. When the police officer takes off his uniform, there is no longer a reason to listen to him.

Reward Power

People in positions of power almost always have the ability to give out rewards. These rewards can include big things like pay raises or promotions and little things like candy or compliments. Giving rewards is indeed sometimes an effective way to manage people but, like Machiavelli's "love," it has serious limitations.

First, rewards are often expensive. Giving everyone in your office a pay raise is a good way to drive your company into bankruptcy. Even giving candy to students becomes a considerable expense for teachers if they aren't careful.

Secondly, the more often you give rewards, the the effective those rewards become. This is a process called **satiation**, and it can make your gifts, your compliments and your presents worthless if you aren't careful. [49]

49 Satiation in behavior analysis. https://appliedbehavioralstrategies.wordpress.com/tag/what-is-satiation/

Satiation: Let's consider the example of chocolate candy. If you perform a task well and I reward you with one small chocolate candy, you will likely feel motivated to continue performing well. However, if I give you a chocolate every time you perform well, you will get tired of chocolate and become less motivated. My chocolate gift will be less and less effective. In order to overcome this, I decide to give you 1 kilogram of chocolate the next time you do well. Unfortunately, if you were tired of chocolate before, if you were satiated, my gift of 1 kilogram of chocolate will make you really tired of chocolate.

As such, if you want your gifts to remain useful, it is good to give them in small quantities. Instead of giving one kilogram of chocolate, you should give one or two grams at a time. This way, the person you are rewarding will always want more chocolate. You should also give rewards inconsistently. For example, I should give you chocolate once every six times you perform well instead of every time. This prevents you from expecting a reward and lowering your motivation.

Relying too much on reward power is unstable because you often can't control the availability of rewards and, if you aren't careful, the value of your rewards will decrease with time.

Coercive Power

This has some similarities to Machiavelli's "fear," although you can have fear without forcing people to do things. Coercion, like fear, becomes problematic when you let it **devolve** into hatred. Coercion is easy to abuse and over-reliance on coercion can make your office or classroom into a very unpleasant place.
The most common type of coer-

cion is punishment. Punishment is absolutely necessary for a leader, but poorly planned or poorly done punishments are dangerous. Like Sun Tzu and the concubines, if you wish to punish your followers, you must ensure you are doing so for clear reasons, to achieve a clear change and in a consistent manner. Random punishments or punishments designed only to show your power will lead very quickly to Machiavelli's hatred.

Overusing coercion also makes it difficult for followers to feel like they **have a stake** in your success. One of the really smart things Sun Tzu did was get the concubines to agree to his leadership. When followers agree to your leadership, they will be much more motivated to help you succeed, they will feel much more ownership for your classroom or office. More motivation means more productivity, more happiness and more success. So, while you must not be afraid to use coercion and punishment, it's important to use these things only as a last resort and only under clear, easy to understand circumstances.

Personal Power Sources

Expert Power

You have expert power when others believe that you are in some way smarter, more rational, stronger or better than the people you lead. This can lead to others trusting and respecting you. Expertise gives your ideas more value than the opinions of others.

Obviously, expert power only works when you actually are an expert. For this reason, a good leader needs to be a lifelong learner and intellectually curious. For example, Dr. McN read widely in the fields of art, philosophy, literature, history and politics. When he spoke, all the students could tell he deserved respect. They could tell this because he legitimately knew more about the world than we did. Other examples of leaders with expert power include Sejong the Great, Steve Jobs, Alexander Hamilton and Queen Elizabeth I of England.

While expertise is an excellent foundation for your power, it is not enough. An expert who is not strong, who has no charisma and who cannot understand how to use rewards and punishments will likely fail. You need to be well rounded.

Referent Power

This is the kind of power that comes from fame or charisma. Referent power comes from your ability to inspire others, to make them feel admiration for you, to identify with you. People like Park Ji-sung or Lee Guk-ju have referent power because of their fame. People like Barack Obama and Neil deGrasse Tyson have referent power (and later fame) because of their charisma. Because of their referent power, these people can influence followers to buy Hyundai cars, vote for a political party or learn about science.

However, unlike expert power, you can get referent power without earning it. People like Kim Kardashian or Jaden Smith, who have a lot of referent power, really didn't do anything to earn that power. They were simply born into famous families. Other people get referent power simply by looking good or having good skills at manipulation. **Conmen** often have a lot of referent power, for example. As such, it is very easy to misuse referent power.

As such, referent power is good, but without expert power and knowledge about how to punish and reward, it can be very empty.

Questions:

Comprehension:

- What is legitimate power?
- What is referent power?
- What is expert power?

Exploration:

- What sorts of power do the worst leaders use? Mediocre leaders? Good leaders?

Activity:

- Choose one of the following and describe how the person uses power. A) Josef Stalin B) Albert Einstein C) Lee Hyo-ri D) Gong Ji-young E) Michael Jordan

Reflection:

- What kinds of power do you use well? What kinds of power do you need to develop? Explain your decisions.

____

____

____

____

____

____

____

____

____

____

25 Theories of Punishment

Main Questions	When was the last time you punished someone?
	Is punishment supposed to make the punisher feel better?
	Is revenge a valid reason to punish someone?
	How long should punishments last?

Vocabulary	Utilitarianism	Retribution
	Deterrence	Rehabilitation
	Free Will	Denounce

There are several theories of how to use punishment to maintain order in a society, in a classroom or in an office. Generally, these theories fall under one of two broad categories, **retributive** and **utilitarian.**[50]

Utilitarian Punishment

Utilitarianism is practical. Under utilitarianism, we only use punishment if that punishment will lead to a positive result. Examples of positive results are deterrence, strengthening the power of social rules or helping the punished person to reform.

The entire purpose of utilitarianism is to maximize happiness. As such, laws in general and punishment in particular are only good if they make the society, school or office happier. As such, because crime, cheating or being lazy hurt happiness, the utilitarian believes we should stop these things. Punishment, then, is justifiable only when it stops laziness, cheating and crime more than it hurts.

Utilitarians, like Machiavelli and Sun Tzu, are "consequentialist." This means they care mostly about the results. They realize that punishment is often bad for the person being punished and for the society. As such, punishment should be carefully limited and only used when it is clearly useful.

An example of this would be releasing a murderer from prison when the murderer gets too old and too sick to be dangerous any more. After all, punishment is only okay if it is serving a purpose, and there is no benefit to punishing a person who can no longer hurt others.

The first kind of good that can come from punishment in utilitarianism is **deterrence**. Deterrence means that punishment will prevent people from committing crime in the future. Deterring the individual is possible, such as when you punish a child so that the child will stop doing bad things. It is also possible to punish as a deterrent to others. For example, if you see a concubine punished for disobeying Sun Tzu, you are much less likely to disobey him in the future.

50 Jrank Articles. http://law.jrank.org/pages/9576/Punishment-THEORIES-PUNISHMENT.html#ixzz3jiAP19HL

Consequentialism says that the results of actions are most important. For example, if you could know 100% that a killer would never kill again, consequentialism says that punishing that person is useless. A good example is Anders Behring Breivik, a Norwegian man who killed 77 people, mostly children. Because Norway has a very utilitarian justice system, if he shows enough improvement, he can rejoin society in 20 years. What do you think?

Rehabilitation is another utilitarian rationale for punishment. The goal of rehabilitation is to prevent future bad behavior by giving offenders the ability to succeed without breaking laws. For example, you might rehabilitate a bad worker by helping him get education or rehabilitate a bad student by helping her get treatment for a mental problem.

Retributive Theory

On the other hand, you can use retributive theory. Under this theory, we punish people because they deserve to be punished. Instead of looking at how to improve things in the future, retribution theory focuses on the past and tries to balance the amount of suffering that the victims and the offenders experienced.

Retribution theory is not concerned with results. A good example of this is Stanley "Tookie" Williams. Williams was convicted of murder as a young man. In prison he reformed and became very useful, negotiating peace between two huge gangs in Los Angeles and helping children escape from gang lifestyles.
However, in order to get retribution, the state of California still executed him.

According to the retributivist, human beings have **free will** and responsibility for their actions. This doesn't apply to insane people or children, but in order to respect the offender's free will we have to punish their crimes. Most simply, retribution is a good way to get revenge. Even the Bible has this reasoning:

"When a man causes a disfigurement in his neighbor, it shall be done to him, fracture for fracture, eye for eye, tooth for tooth."

Also, a retributivist might feel that she is expressing **denunciation** - showing the criminal how much society is angry at them. This is kind of a mix of retribution and utilitarian thinking.

Questions:

Comprehension:

- What is retribution?
- What is utilitarianism?

Exploration:

- What sorts of punishments are best for leaders to use, retributive or utilitarian?
- How can punishments backfire, in your experience?
- The danger of utilitarianism is mostly that others will not accept it as valid. The danger of retribution is that it easily becomes revenge. How can you avoid these problems?

Project:

- Consider the following scenario with two other students. A 16 year old child has just been caught stealing a bicycle from her school. The first student should design a strategy for a teacher punishing the child. The second student should design a strategy for a parent punishing the child. The third student should design a punishment strategy for a police officer.

The Ken Ham vs. Bill Nye Debate

26

Scientist and inventor Bill Nye, left, debated CEO and religious museum owner Ken Ham, right.

Main Questions	How good are you at persuading others?
	Is logic the most important part of persuasion?
	Is it possible to lose an argument when you have better facts?
	How important is emotion in persuasion?

Vocabulary	Fossil	Irrelevant
	Creationism	Condescension
	Secular	Self-depreciation

On February 4th, 2014, respected scientist, inventor and TV presenter Bill Nye debated religious museum operator Ken Ham[51]. Mr. Nye was arguing that the biological theory of evolution is real. He had thousands of pages of data on **fossils**, genetics and the weight of virtually all of the scientific community. Mr. Ham was a creationist. A creationist believes that the world is 6,000 years old, all animals alive today were created 4,000 years ago and that evolution is an illusion. Very few Christians, or religious people in general, are creationists. Mr. Ham supported his argument with an unusual interpretation of the Bible and basically nothing else. He also admitted that no amount of evidence would ever change his opinion.

What struck me, watching the debate, is how much better Mr. Nye's evidence and logic was, but also how much better Mr. Ham was at the emotional parts of persuasion. Let's look at how Mr. Ham and Mr. Nye try to persuade us to explore how they failed and succeeded.

1. Mr. Nye starts his speech with a joke, but it falls flat. This has the effect of making him look weaker. Logically, it's **irrelevant**, but emotionally this is very important.
2. Mr. Nye admits that the question of evolution vs. **creation** is a battle of stories. This is absolutely true, but it makes his facts look like they are only opinions. Once again, this is logically irrelevant and even admirably honest, but emotionally it makes Mr. Nye's position weaker.
3. Mr. Nye appears to think that Mr. Ham's "silly" opinions mean that Mr. Ham is also "silly." In other words, he dangerously underestimates Mr. Ham. This causes a number of huge problems for the goal of persuasion. First, Mr. Nye seems completely unprepared for Mr. Ham's "observational vs historical science" idea. The audience interprets this as evidence that "observational and historical science" is a real thing. Much more damagingly, Mr. Nye is visibly struggling to remain respectful. He tries and fails to hide a bit of **condescension**. He refers to himself as "a real scientist" and "a reasonable man" several times. This comes across as arrogant. It is almost impossible to persuade people you are condescending to.
4. Mr. Nye calls creationism a dangerous trend that will make the United States weak. This is probably true, but by attacking the creationists in the audience and calling them a "force for weakness," Mr. Nye is making them defensive and much less likely to listen. He also indirectly attacks pastors

51 https://www.youtube.com/watch?v=ZOJkl4Agf4c

and education in the state of Kentucky (the debate was in Kentucky), to the irritation of his audience.

5. Mr. Nye clearly has a limited knowledge of the Bible. This shouldn't be a problem, since they are discussing evolution, but Mr. Nye forgets that for the audience, the Bible is a much more reliable source of truth than science. This is unfortunate, because if Mr. Nye had known more about the Bible, he could have attacked Mr. Ham in the religious terms that the audience understands best. Mr. Ham's understanding of the Bible is not very well thought out, so Mr. Nye could have really beaten him badly in this area.

By comparison, while Mr. Ham's logical arguments were a disaster, he did a better job of emotional persuasion. Let's look over some of the strategies Mr. Ham used to, in essence, try to overcome the weight of science.

1. Mr. Ham is very good at **self-depreciation**, or the art of making himself look humble. As opposed to Mr. Nye's barely hidden contempt, Mr. Ham' s humility invites the audience and online viewers to get comfortable. He repeatedly says that "**secularists**" believe that "man is the ultimate authority, I don't." This humility says "I'm not going to attack you."
2. Mr. Ham creates enemies for the audience. From a logical standpoint, this is ridiculous. Science and creationism are theories to explain the world, they cannot be good or evil. However, people tend to understand most things in terms of good and evil. Mr. Ham recognizes this and tells us about the evil conspiracy of "secularists" and "the media" who are keeping the truth hidden. He also equates Darwinism with Social Darwinism, which is a theory to justify racism.[52] Effectively, he is saying "evolution will make you into an immoral racist."
3. Mr. Ham understands that fear, in this case the fear of death, is much stronger than logic. As such, he explains that believing in evolution means that you must not believe in heaven. He goes on to explain that believing in evolution makes your life meaningless. This is logically nonsense, but on an emotional level, very powerful.
4. "Admit the belief." While Mr. Nye never seems to understand that creationists believe the Bible more than science, Mr. Ham immediately recognizes that evolutionists believe science more than the Bible. As such, he makes arguments for secularists on secular terms. In order to persuade, you must do so on your target's terms.

52 Social Darwinism http://www.allaboutscience.org/what-is-social-darwinism-faq.htm

Questions:

Exploration:

- Logic is important for persuasion, but it is not the only part of persuasion. What, in your opinion, are the most important things?
- Pretend you are Mr. Nye. How would you persuade the young earth creationists that evolution is valid? If you were Mr. Ham, how would you try to convince mainstream scientists that evolution is wrong?
- When are the best times to try persuading someone else?

Project:

- Research the techniques used by salesmen to persuade customers. What do they emphasize?

____

____

____

____

____

____

____

____

____

____

How to Persuade People

27

Main Questions	How can you persuade an enemy?
	Why is listening important for persuasion?
	Can you overpower an opponent with your logic and facts?
	How should you use empathy in persuasion?

Vocabulary	Intimidation	Investment
	Hysteria	Consumer
	Hostage	Rabid
	Ambitious	

Many people are really, shockingly bad at persuasion. Think of your family gatherings when your aunts and uncles, parents and cousins discuss politics or religion. While the aunts and uncles would very much like to persuade each other that one view is correct, how often have you seen them succeed? In my family at least, this sort of successful persuasion has literally never happened.

So, why? The first and most important reason is simply the fact that persuasion is really hard. As you learned in Chapter 16, people all have confirmation bias. That is, people like their opinions and don't like to change. They dislike new evidence and they often find disagreements annoying. Some people are open minded some of the time but, honestly, not very many and not very often.

The second reason is that most people, when they try to persuade, use really, really bad technique. They use **intimidation** when they should be comforting, they use logic when they should be using empathy and use insults when they should be listening. Let's look at some specific tips and tricks you can use to persuade your students, employees and even bosses.

Understand Why Persuasion Is Hard

The first thing to really think about is what persuasion means. When you persuade, your goal is to change someone else's opinion. This is difficult to do in any circumstance but, interestingly, it's even harder when you're trying to persuade an intelligent person. Intelligent people typically have a lot of confidence in their opinions and a lot of experience being correct. Often, they will stop listening to you very quickly.

This should not stop you from trying, though. According to Dr. Steven Novella, there is almost no relationship between **certainty** and accuracy.[53] I want to emphasize this. When you meet a person who is very sure about something, this does not mean they are more likely to be correct. During the dilemma section, we talked before about how strong beliefs make for bad conversations, but they also make for bad thinking and horrible persuasion. I really recommend you limit your strong beliefs as much as possible if you want to be a good leader.

53 Certainty vs. accuracy. http://www.thegreatcourses.com/courses/your-deceptive-mind-a-scientific-guide-to-critical-thinking-skills.html

There's also the problem of intellectual **investment**. Really intelligent people spend a lot of time thinking. Thinking about an issue is a type of investment and the more a person has invested in an opinion, the slower they are going to be to change their belief.

Realize That Persuasion Is Not Primarily Logical

I'd like you to imagine a scenario. Let's say Jane likes fish more than beef and wants to convince John to eat fish instead of beef. Imagine you are John as Jane makes the following, truthful, argument.

Beef is wasteful and every time you eat beef you are hurting the environment! Cows are so inefficient to raise that they destroy acres of wilderness! Their farts - yes, they fart constantly! - poison the air and cause global warming! If you eat beef instead of fish you are basically saying "I hate the environment!"

Jane has basically no chance to succeed in this argument. Even though everything she said about the environment is true, John is significantly more likely to insult her than listen to her opinion. This is because Jane's presentation of the argument was hostile, condescending and **hysterical**.

Levitt and Dubner, authors of the Freakonomics series of books, explain:

"Whenever you set out to persuade someone, remember that you are merely the producer of the argument. The **consumer** has the only vote that counts. Your argument may be factually indisputable and logically airtight but if it doesn't resonate for the recipient, you won't get anywhere. "

In other words, when you try to persuade you are much less a philosopher or logic expert than you are a salesman. Proving the other person is wrong is not the point in persuasion. Demonstrating how smart you are is not the goal. The only goal is to change their opinion and in order to do that, you will need to "sell" them an appealing alternative.

Genuinely Listen

The FBI has a dedicated group of professionals whose job is to negotiate for the release of **hostages**. When an angry person holds his or her family hostage with a knife, one of these hostage negotiators will come to help end the situation peacefully. When a terrorist kidnaps a group of nightclub patrons, it is a hostage negotiator who tries to get the people out safely.

If you really think about it, these hostage negotiators are professional persuaders working in the most difficult conceivable situations. After all, their job is to persuade the criminal or terrorist to change their strong original belief - "I should kill or harm these people" - into a completely new and totally opposite belief - "it' s best if I give up peacefully."

According to the FBI's hostage negotiation guidebook, the first thing you should do is ask the terrorist or criminal to explain their point of view. You shouldn't start with your own opinion, you shouldn't make demands, you should listen.

Ask the person you want to persuade open ended questions and actively listen. For example, you should say things like "I really want to understand where you are coming from. Could you explain?" or "I'm curious why you think so."
When the person is talking, you should continue actively listening. You should

These people were freed from Iran by hostage negotiators.

avoid arguing or analyzing their thoughts. Instead of saying "that's not true" you should instead say "interesting, how does that work?"

When the person makes good points, and almost everyone will make good points, you should acknowledge their good points. It's important to remember that very few people have stupid beliefs. When a person believes something, they almost always have good reasons and you should be respectful enough to admit this.

Build Empathy

After you've actively listened to the other person's story, try to genuinely understand the emotional reasons the other person has for believing as they do. If, for example, your uncle believes that we should all carry AK47 rifles on the subway, you should really try to understand where this opinion came from. This is a pretty extreme opinion, but there are dozens of understandable, emotional reasons he might have for wanting to take AK47s on the subway.

Maybe he once used an AK47 to chase away a robber in a subway station. Or maybe he is afraid that a terrorist could kill unarmed people on the subway. Maybe he failed to protect his army friend from a **rabid** dog because he didn't have his AK47. All of these reasons could lead to his opinion and, if you want to change his mind, you need to understand them.[54]

Build Trust

After you have genuinely empathized with the person you want to persuade, it's time to build trust with that person. This means you need to make them feel safe. You need to convince them to lower their defenses and you need to convince them that you are not a threat.

The reason for this is that our brains are basically built in layers. The oldest lay-

54 FBI hostage negotiation techniques http://time.com/38796/6-hostage-negotiation-techniques-that-will-get-you-what-you-want/

er is what some scientists call the "lizard brain." This part of our brains is about threats, fighting or running away. When you see a car coming to run you over, for example, your lizard brain will take over your body and you will run away without thinking. This is useful and we need the lizard brain, but when the lizard brain is in control, people think more like lizards and less like human beings.

The reason you should build trust is that you are basically calming the lizard brain down, soothing it and letting the person's higher brain take over. This step is not optional. If you don't calm down the lizard, you will never get to talk with the person.

Don't Pretend Your Argument Is Perfect

Let me say this frankly, your argument will never be perfect. It won't be perfect if you study for a hundred years, it will not be perfect if you practice every day and it will not be perfect if angels come from heaven to help you. Everything has flaws.

As such, you should be honest that your argument is not perfect. Doing so will go a long ways toward making the other person trust you. It also means that you might learn something new.

No Insults

It might feel really good to insult your opponent. The opponent might be nasty or dumb or lazy or whatever. You might feel like you are punishing them with retributive justice.

However, you need to know that as soon as you use an insult, you have turned on your opponent's lizard brain, destroyed any trust you have built, undermined any empathy you have and made listening impossible. In other words, insults equal guaranteed failure if you want to persuade someone.

Use Narrative

Like we learned in Ch. 11, narrative is an incredibly powerful tool. It's no different in persuasion. You should use all the same narrative skills you learned earlier to create not just a logical argument, but an emotional argument.

Let's use Jane's fish vs. beef example again, but this time with good narrative and a focus on emotional persuasion.

"Hey John, would you like to come to my party? I'm going to be baking salmon in lemon and butter. I learned how to make a special sweet orange sauce that I'm going to put on top and I have some fresh black pepper I'll sprinkle over the sauce. Trust me, you will enjoy this more than a hamburger."

Notice that this argument has none of the logical points of the earlier attempt. Jane does not mention the environment, she does not give statistics or information, she just appeals to John's senses. This will not completely convince John to stop eating beef, but it is a first step, which brings us to the next point.

Be Patient

One of the easiest ways to fail in persuasion is to be too **ambitious**. If Jane wants to persuade John to stop eating beef, she should start by convincing him to have fish instead of beef for one or two meals. Then, after John is comfortable with Jane and with eating fish, Jane should suggest that "maybe you should eat less beef. I hear there are environmental problems with cows." If John accepts this, Jane should wait longer until John is comfortable eating much less beef. Then, maybe a few months after she began, Jane should suggest John stop eating beef altogether.

When Jane tries to convince John of everything - eat fish right now, beef is bad for the environment, you should stop eating beef - all at one time, she is very, very unlikely to succeed.

Questions:

Comprehension:

- What is a lizard brain?
- Is persuasion primarily about logic?
- Are smart people easier or harder to persuade?

Exploration:

- Explain a time when you successfully persuaded someone to change a belief? How did you do it?
- What stumbling blocks most affect your teachers or bosses?
- What strategies will you use most often to persuade your followers?
- Why is it so hard to persuade someone when you are angry?

Project:

- Go back and analyze the Bill Nye and Ken Ham debate. Compare your notes with a friend.

Supplemental chapter

Getting a Job Overseas

Main Questions	How can you impress your future boss?
	How is the job interview process different overseas?
	What are some traps and dangers in a job interview?
	How can you make it difficult for a boss to reject you?

Vocabulary	Dead fish handshake	Secretary
	Basement	Morale
	Deflect	

Part One, How the Process Works

Getting a job is one of the most important tasks you will face in your life. It is how you transition from the life of a dependent student to the life of an independent adult. Therefore, it's important to know what to expect from your interviewers.

The first part of the process is called the pre-interview. This is everything involving your resume, your cover letter and any papers the employer wants you to fill out. Sometimes, this also includes a phone interview.

This is mostly about finding people who meet the minimum requirements. For example, the employer will often use the pre-interview phase for eliminating the applicants who don't have enough education, people who aren't qualified or people who are obviously not good employees. This means that when you get to the face to face interview, you are probably already one of the best applicants.

Most interviews take place on the company's property. I have experienced job interviews in large warehouses, in an empty classroom, in tall office buildings, in the boss's office and one time in a **basement.**

Most of these interviews are face to face with one person. However, I have also experienced interviews where one company representative interviewed 6 applicants at one time and another where I, alone, had to answer questions from 4 interviewers. Before this happens, you will probably meet a **secretary** or assistant. I strongly recommend you are nice to this person.

Most interviews begin with the interviewer greeting you and making some small talk. You can take this opportunity to relax, take hints from the environment and make a good impression on your boss. Usually after 30 seconds to a couple of minutes, the interviewer will move onto the more serious questions.

Often employers will want to check and clarify the things on your resume. If you said that you graduated high school with a perfect score, for example, the interviewer might ask you how you accomplished such an amazing score. Often, they will also check your job history and ask questions about why you quit your old jobs. This is to check the accuracy of your resume and clarify anything confusing.

After checking and clarifying your resume and application papers, interviews often move onto questions designed to test you. Employers will often ask you to solve scenarios related to your job. For example, when I interviewed for a job in politics, my interviewers asked me to make a plan for dealing with a foreign country while working with a team. In another interview for a teaching position, the interviewers asked me to teach a demonstration class.

However, it's not always so complicated. Sometimes, the employer will simply ask what you would do in a situation. For example, "what would you do if a customer was angry and threatened to sue the company?"

Another category of questions centers on how you have behaved in the past. For example, an employer might ask how you behaved the last time you had a difficult deadline or how you solved conflicts with coworkers in the past. The generic version of this is "what was the hardest challenge you faced at your last job and how did you overcome it?"

After the interviewer has finished asking questions about your past, behavior and strategies, they will commonly ask if you have any questions about the company. Don't be shy. If you don't know where the offices are, ask to see the offices. If you wonder about the hours, ask. If you aren't sure what the company's strategy is, ask the interviewer to clarify.

Once the interview has finished, the interviewer probably won't say if you got the job or not. When you leave the interview, you can take the opportunity to collect business cards, thank the secretaries and assistants and look over the workplace.

It usually takes the company a couple days to decide whether or not they will hire you, but sometimes it can take several weeks. If the interviews were very competitive, they might even ask you to return for a second interview.

Part Two, Questions From the Employer's Perspective

Most employers will get more applications than they can possibly accept. This means they almost always look for reasons to eliminate applicants. This is important to remember, the employer is looking for excuses to reject you.

In addition to having more applicants than jobs, companies face a lot of risk when they hire a new person. A really bad hire can cost tens of thousands of dollars in salary, training costs, and wasted time. A bad new employee will take up management time, hurt **morale** and lower the productivity of other employees.

As such, most of the questions employers are likely to ask you during the interview are designed to eliminate bad applicants. Let's look at some of these questions and techniques.

1. *Asking you to explain how you fit into the company.* Most employers publicize information about themselves. They have websites and pamphlets you can find online. The question "how do you fit here" really means "have you done your homework and researched us" in many cases. A vague or silly answer will tell the employer you haven't done any research or preparation. This is a very easy way to get eliminated.

   Solution - Do your homework. Learn about the employer before you come to the interview.

2. *Asking you to complain about past employers.* This is when the employer asks about the things you didn't like in your past job. If you've never had a professional job, they might ask what you disliked most about your school. This is designed to make you say negative things. "I really hated how my boss always made me use a stupid filing system." If you were unhappy with your previous job, you will probably be unhappy in your new job. Bosses don't like unhappy employees.

   Solution - Answer by telling the boss ways your old employer could have been more efficient. Instead of complaining about the filing system, for example, say something like "I thought the filing system was inefficient. I suggested a more efficient (specific system) and here are the details of that system."

3. *Asking about your biggest weakness*. This question is almost always a trap. When the employer asks "what is your biggest weakness" they are really saying "give me an excuse to reject you." You might be tempted to give an honest answer "my biggest weakness is organization." This will get you rejected.

Solution - You shouldn't lie, but you should **deflect** the question. My biggest weakness really is organization, but in an interview I should say something like "I used to struggle with organization but these days I'm using the planning program in my phone to organize my life more efficiently."

4. *Asking what your biggest challenge was* - This question is designed to eliminate people who see themselves as victims. Victims don't like to take responsibility; they are passive and destructive for an employer. When the employer asks about your biggest challenge, they are trying to see if you took responsibility or blamed others. Blaming others for your challenges is an easy way to get rejected.

Solution - You are not a victim. You can take responsibility for the things that happen around you. If other people are able to push you around and ruin your projects, you need to be stronger. Keep this in mind and take responsibility for the problems you've faced.

5. *Asking about your future plans* - This is a strategy for eliminating applicants with no long term goals. Most employers would prefer to hire someone who plans to stay with the company for 20 years than someone who just needs a job temporarily. Being vague or silly in your answer is a good way to get rejected.

Solution - Dream big and fill those dreams with lots of details.

6. *Asking about your best experiences at your last job/at school* - This question is designed to eliminate applicants who don't actually care about their work. Answering this question with something silly like "we had free coffee" tells the employer you didn't actually care about your last job.

Solution - Explain the meaningful things you get out of your work or studies. For example, my best experiences at my current job are watching as students discover new concepts, new ways of thinking. I love this experience and I would feel incomplete if it stopped happening. I care deeply about my work and that feeling is one reason I care. You should have a similar experience.

7. *Asking about your previous responsibilities* - This question basically means "were you a robot or did you actively help the company?" A very dry or boring answer here indicates that you will not be a very dynamic employee.

Solution - Focus on the creative or exceptional things you've done at your jobs or in school. Talk about the soccer team you organized or the school newspaper you wrote for. Employers like active employees.

8. *Asking about your greatest strengths* - Almost all important jobs require confidence. If you don't know what your own strengths are, you probably aren't very confident. A meek employee will often not meet a company's needs and thus a bad answer can get you rejected.

Solution - Talk frankly about your successes, but also give credit to supervisors, teachers and coworkers who helped you.

9. *Asking what makes you special* - In the English speaking world, very few employers want a "normal" or "average" employee. Normal and average employees do not give their employers any special advantages. Saying "I' m just a normal person," as many of the applicants I've interviewed have said, is an excellent way to get rejected.

Solution - Do interesting things and don't be afraid to talk about them. If you know how to train dogs, for example, you can explain how your knowledge gives you special insight into behavior. Or, if you can build a computer, it gives you an opportunity to explain how computer building helps you think systematically. Most Western companies want their employees to have "big" lives outside of work. In fact, many companies think that applicants who don't have outside hobbies and interests are likely **dispassionate** and unproductive.

10. *Asking what the most courageous thing you've done at work is* - Employers want employees who are strong and courageous enough to try difficult

tasks. Applicants who are too timid or meek are unlikely to take new opportunities or lead new initiatives when they become employees. If you' ve never done something that required courage, you will probably get rejected.

Solution - Courage doesn't have to be about fighting lions or jumping out of airplanes. Talk about being the first person in your family to get a master' s degree or how you applied to a poetry club even though you didn't know anyone who wrote poetry.

11. *Asking how you work on a team* - Most jobs will require you to work with others. When an employer asks how you work on a team they are really asking "are you going to fight with my other employees?" If you don't have specific examples of successfully working on a team, you are likely to get rejected.

Solution - If you don't already have experience working with a team, get some. If you do have experience working on a team, make sure you can give specific examples of making that team better.

12. *Asking how you handle stress* - This is similar to asking you to complain about your previous boss. If you answer that you cry, panic or demand to leave, you are very likely to get rejected.

Solution - Employers like strong employees, not weaklings or victims. You should explain how you keep calm and rational during difficult times.

13. *Asking why you left your old job* - This obviously isn't a problem for new college graduates, but if you're leaving an old job for a new one, you need to have a good answer. The real meaning of this question is "are you going to abandon my company?"

Solution - Don't say anything bad about your old boss. Instead, focus on the opportunities in the new job and focus on the positive changes in your life. For example, I left my previous job because the boss didn't pay his employees on time. However, when I explained this to my new employers I said "I learned a lot at (old company) but I am excited to move onto a career with more stability and greater opportunity."

14. *Asking if you have questions* - This question is obviously an opportunity for you to learn more about the company, but it also shows your interest. If you haven't prepared a list of questions for the interviewer, it shows you aren't very interested in the job.

Solution - Do your homework. Ask the interviewer interesting and intelligent questions. Ask to take a tour of the office and ask if you can meet the other people in the office. This makes it much harder for the company to reject you.

Part Three, Cultural Differences

There are major differences in culture between the cultural West and Korea and those differences extend into job interviews. This isn't as big a problem as you probably think, but there are some general strategies you can use to succeed in Western job interviews.

So, why aren't cultural differences always a big deal? The truth is that your interviewer will know you are foreign. If you do something strange, they will probably just assume it is part of your culture. As such, it's probably not worth your time to practice "acting American/Canadian/British." However, there are some things you can do to overcome cultural differences.

a) *Be friendly* - It's not that hard to overcome cultural problems with a friendly person. If you are open, smile a lot and listen to others, the cultural differences between you and your new company can be resolved with minimal stress.

b) *Be open* - You don't have to pretend you are a native of the USA/Canada/England, but you should show that you are willing to adapt to their traditions. "I don't know, but I'm willing to learn" is a great attitude for a job applicant to have. Don't insist on doing things the Korean way when you work overseas. "When in Rome, do as the Romans."

c) *Remember that you do not represent - Korea* Very few people in the English-speaking world will see you as a representative of Korea. They will see you as an individual who just happens to have come from Korea. Even more important, do not act as if you need to spread Korean culture to your new job. People will ask you about Korea and they will ask you for ideas, but do not try to force your culture on others.

d) *Don't have too many restrictions* - Companies will ask you to do many, many tasks. The more of these tasks you can perform the better. An employee who needs special food, a special kind of office, special music or special supervision is less valuable than a flexible employee who will do anything.

So, what are the biggest cultural differences you are likely to see? The biggest is emphasis. In Western countries, employers tend not to care about your school scores. As long as you graduated from college, your test scores and class grades really aren't important. Where in Korea employers commonly spend the interview asking about TOEIC and school grades, I have literally never been asked about my grades in an interview. Instead, employers will focus on how quickly you can think, how independent you are and how good your attitude is.

Further, I recommend you focus on appearing confident. Don't apologize unless you've done something wrong. Korean manners can sometimes seem very submissive to Westerners. Look your employer in the eye, speak clearly and sit straight. You may bow if you like. This will be a little bit unusual, but most Westerners will probably like it.

One thing Westerners will not like is the "**dead fish handshake**." This is when someone gives a super soft handshake. In Western countries, this is considered disrespectful. Don't hurt the other person's hand, but when you give a handshake, be firm and strong.

Dedication

Any project as large as a book is going to be the result of collaboration and this textbook is no exception. I would like to sincerely thank Professor Kyeong-ae Choi for her help and guidance in getting this book published. Chris Marsh endured hours of my harebrained ideas and provided copy editing. Thanks also to my mother, Kat Garrido and sister, Natalia Garrido, for their support and guidance.

I would also like to thank my bosses, Professor Young-ju Jeon and Professor Jong-bok Lee for giving me the freedom to pursue my own curriculum and the encouragement when I needed time to experiment.

Most of all, I would like to thank all of the students who've taken my English Conversation classes. This book is the result of experimenting with dozens of ideas in class. Thank you, students, for enduring my experiments. I hope they were not too painful.

- Ben

Author Information:

Ben Garrido is the author of the novels The Blackguard and The Potency (available soon). He also writes award winning journalism for the Reno News and Review, Chico News and Review and others, and lectures on second language acquisition at Mokwon University in South Korea. His other textbook, also published by Shinasa, is "Origins of Anglo-American Culture." He writes on subjects including language, fiction, adventure and logic on his website, www.bengarrido.com. Raised in Reno, Nevada, he now divides his time between South Korea and the United States.

Critical Thinking For Leaders

First Published Dec. 2016
SHINASA Publishing Co.
4, Tongil-ro 59-gil, Eunpyeong-gu, Seoul, Korea
Registered : 9-52 (Jan. 5 1956)
Tel: 02-382-6411
Fax: 02-382-6401
E-mail: shinasa@hanmail.net
Homepage: www.shinasa.co.kr

ISBN : 978-89-8396-963-7(93740)
Printed and bounded in Korea

₩ 15000